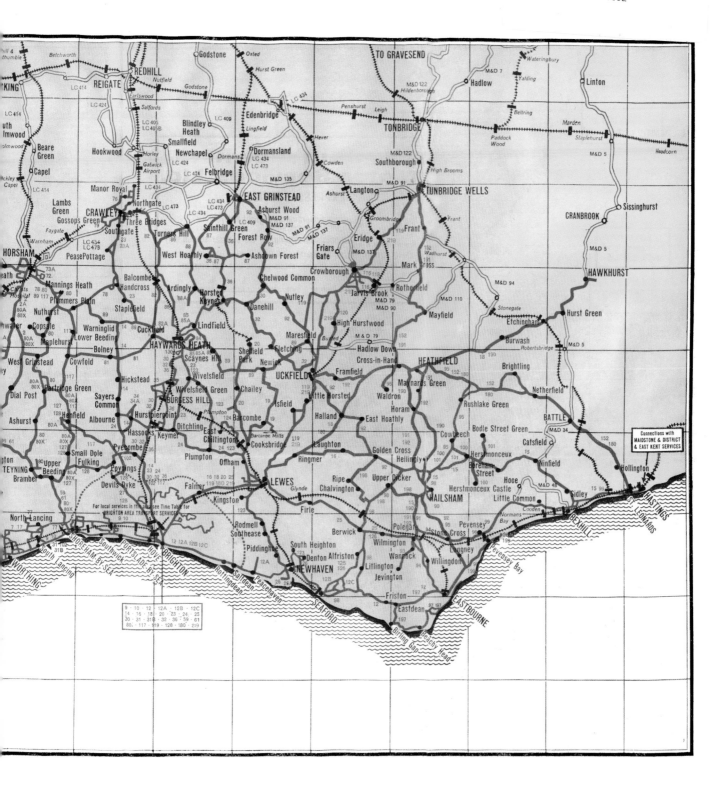

SOUTHDOWN
in NBC days

Glyn Kraemer-Johnson and John Bishop

Ian Allan
PUBLISHING

CONTENTS

**Narrative by Glyn Kraemer-Johnson
Photographs selected and captioned by John Bishop**

First published 2008

ISBN (10) 0 7110 3254 8
ISBN (13) 978 0 7110 3254 5

Published by Ian Allan Publishing
an imprint of Ian Allan Publishing Ltd, Hersham, Surrey, KT12 4RG

Printed in England by Ian Allan Printing Ltd, Hersham, Surrey, KT12 4RG

Code: 0804/B1

Visit the Ian Allan Publishing website
at www.ianallanpublishing.com

INTRODUCTION

FOR MANY it epitomised the bus industry at its lowest ebb. It was a time when well-loved liveries and many long-established names disappeared. It was a time when staff morale was at an all-time low, when employees used to working for a company with local pride found themselves employed by a faceless organisation 'somewhere up there' in which they were little more than a number. It was a time of staff and vehicle shortages, with consequent daily lists of cancelled services, and it was a time when enthusiasts mourned the passing of individual vehicle-purchasing policies, the Bristol VR double-decker and Leyland National single-decker becoming the staple fare throughout England and Wales. I refer, of course, to the reign of the National Bus Company.

It was also a time of dwindling traffic, diminishing profits and, consequently, of reduced services. Radical action was necessary to halt or at least slow down the decline, and this was achieved largely by the spread and ultimately the almost universal adoption of one-man operation (OMO), as it was originally known. However, this did not find favour with the travelling public, resulting as it did in longer waiting times at bus stops, the inability to board an empty bus at termini and the loss of the friendly conductor to help the elderly and with shopping and push-chairs. Given that the introduction of OMO coincided largely with the birth of the National Bus Company, many probably saw NBC as being responsible for the decline in service, a criticism that was unjustified. Such measures would have been necessary in any case and indeed were also being introduced by the municipal and independent sectors.

Vehicles too were changing. The rear engine was becoming universally adopted, initially because there was a school of thought that higher-capacity vehicles meant that frequencies could be cut without a reduction in the number of available seats. Of course, the ability of a rear-engined bus to have the entrance beside the driver made the layout ideal for one-man operation, and thus the fate of the half-cab double-decker was sealed.

However, it was not all negative. There were innovations, and in its 19-year existence NBC did much to shape the industry as we know it today.

Since the late 'Forties the industry had been divided into four groups. There were the independents, mainly the smaller concerns that were privately owned, and there were the municipally-owned fleets, whose policies were dictated by the Transport Committee of the local council. Then there were the two major groups, which shared the majority of the rest of the country. Firstly there was the Tilling Group, which had been nationalised since 1948 and which had introduced a fairly high degree of standardisation. Liveries were generally red or green with cream bands (although there were exceptions), and the vehicles operated were mainly the products of the Government-owned concerns of Bristol Commercial Vehicles and Eastern Coach Works. Finally there was the British Electric Traction Co. BET had been split from the Tilling Group in 1942 and had thus avoided nationalisation. Unlike Tilling it allowed its subsidiaries to maintain individual liveries and to follow their own vehicle-purchasing policies. One of BET's subsidiaries was Southdown Motor Services Ltd of Brighton.

Despite falling receipts BET had managed to retain its bus interests, but in 1967 it finally succumbed to pressure and sold out to the Transport Holding Co, owner of the Tilling Group. Under the Transport Act 1968 was formed the National Bus Company, into which were incorporated all the former Tilling and BET subsidiaries, including Southdown.

One of the first steps taken by the NBC was to rationalise the areas covered by its subsidiaries and to merge some of the smaller companies with their larger neighbours. Although Southdown's Head Office was in Brighton, local services in the town were operated by the Brighton, Hove & District Omnibus Co, a Tilling Group company that could scarcely have been much more 'Tilling', being the direct successor to the Brighton operations of Thomas Tilling Ltd. Under the rationalisation of companies it was logical that the 150-vehicle fleet should come under Southdown control, and on 31 December 1968 BH&D ceased to exist.

Thus the stage was set for 19 years of NBC control.

Telling fellow enthusiasts that we were writing this book has generally met with groans, but, love it or loathe it, the NBC era saw many changes in the bus industry, some good, some not so good, but all of which deserve to be recorded. We have not attempted to write a concise history of Southdown under NBC ownership, but a story in pictures and words of the company's development throughout the period and the foundations that were laid for the privatised and deregulated companies that were to follow.

Glyn Kraemer-Johnson
Hailsham, East Sussex
January 2008

1

QUIET BEGINNINGS

AS IS so often the case with mergers and takeovers there were initially few outward signs of change, and those that there were affected the former Brighton, Hove & District operations more than those of the main Southdown fleet. Naturally enough, ex-BH&D vehicles had Southdown legal lettering applied and in June 1969 were renumbered by the addition of 2000 to their fleet numbers. The general public, however, was probably completely unaware of any difference.

Both Southdown and BH&D had resisted the rear-engined bus until the summer of 1968, when both operators took delivery of Bristol RESL6G single-deckers, the Bristol chassis by then being available on the open market. However, BH&D had placed an order for 10 Bristol VR double-deckers, and these were delivered to Southdown after the merger. They were painted in traditional BH&D red and cream livery and carried Brighton Hove & District fleetnames but were registered in the County Borough of Brighton as OCD 763-72G, Hove-based BH&D having registered its vehicles in East Sussex.

The following year saw Southdown take delivery of the first of its own VRs, bringing with them the first signs of lowering standards, for they were basically the normal Bristol/ECW product and, indeed, had been ordered by BH&D. In exchange the BH&D fleet received ten 33ft Daimler Fleetlines with dual-door Northern Counties body-work featuring traditional Southdown interiors with higher-backed seats and wood-grain effect Formica on seat backs and side panels. Painted in red and cream with BH&D fleetnames, they looked superb. Fifteen similar Fleetlines, painted in traditional apple green and primrose, were taken into the main Southdown fleet, but these were to the shorter, 30ft length and had single-door Northern Counties

bodies. Indeed, it would seem fairly safe to assume that, had the NBC not come into being, Southdown — despite its long association with Leyland —would have adopted the Northern Counties-bodied Fleetline as standard. In 1971 a further 15 were delivered to the BH&D fleet — again 33ft long with dual-door bodywork but this time with Leyland (rather than Gardner) engines; again they were finished in full BH&D livery.

Also in 1971— perhaps inevitably — a start was made on painting the ex-BH&D vehicles in apple green and primrose with '**SOUTHDOWN-B-H&D**' fleetnames. Although very smart, the Lodekkas never looked quite right in their new colours. Convertible open-toppers, however, retained their traditional cream and black livery, albeit with the addition of the new-style fleetname.

The BH&D fleet at the time of takeover had been 100% Bristol and, apart from the REs, was totally non-standard to Southdown. Moreover the fleet included some 60 rear-entrance Bristol KS and KSW types. With the standardisation of the livery in 1971, Southdown began to apply '**SOUTHDOWN-B-H&D**' fleetnames to some of its standard Northern Counties-bodied Leyland PD3 'Queen Mary' double-deckers, which were then transferred to the Brighton operation. These, together with the newly delivered vehicles, allowed the withdrawal of most of the K types, and by the end of 1971 only a handful remained.

Bristol chassis, in the form of more RE saloons and VR double-deckers, now constituted the bulk of new deliveries. Fifteen VRs delivered in 1972 had dual-door bodywork, for use on local routes in Brighton. Ten were allocated to the

In the early months of NBC's existence little change was apparent. Only the legal lettering reveals that BH&D Bristol KSW6G 461 (HAP 999), seen at Mill House, Portslade, on 18 May 1969, was now part of the Southdown fleet. Completing a football-pools coupon was once a popular Saturday activity. Chris Warren

ex-BH&D garages at Conway Street and Whitehawk, displacing the original BH&D VRs, which were repainted green and cream and shipped off to Portsmouth; the other five were allocated initially to the main Southdown fleet at Edward Street, but the Southdown crews did not favour the dual-door layout, and they soon joined the other 10 on BH&D routes. The same year saw the arrival of the final 15 Daimler Fleetlines, again with Leyland engines but with bodywork by Eastern Coach Works. The 1972 deliveries were the first — and, as it turned out, only — new vehicles to feature the revised fleetname style and were also the last to arrive in traditional Southdown colours.

With Daimler and Bristol now the choice for stage-carriage vehicles, it was left to the coaching fleet to carry on the Leyland connection, and here the Leopard reigned supreme. A batch of 30 Leopards with rather unusual Northern Counties dual-purpose bodies had been delivered in 1969. Very high and very heavy, they were nonetheless very comfortable and were finished in a semi-

coach livery of apple green with a dark-green waistband. In the event they seemed to spend most of their time on stage-carriage work.

As for the 'pure' coaches, gone were the days of the much-favoured Beadle and Harrington bodies, both manufacturers having ceased production. In fact the building of British coach bodies was now pretty much limited to Duple and Plaxton. Southdown took examples of both for its tour fleet, Duple supplying 20 very impressive Commander-bodied Leopards in 1970, Plaxton following suit in 1971 with its popular 'Panorama Elite'. The latter, 25 in number, would be the last new coaches delivered in Southdown green.

Right: **Ex-BH&D Bristol KSW6G/ECW 2477 (KAP 551)** poses inside the east garage at Conway Street, Hove, on 23 September 1972. By this time the last K types had been withdrawn from normal service, 2477's survival being due to its demotion in November 1970 to a driver trainer — a role it would continue to perform until March 1977. Chris Warren

Right: **The majority of the fleet taken over with BH&D comprised Bristol Lodekkas, and these included 15 of the less-common FSF variant combining the standard wheelbase with a forward entrance. With a backdrop of Brighton's Regency buildings, Bristol-engined 2027 (TPN 27), formerly BH&D 27, was photographed at the Black Rock end of Marine Parade on 4 September 1971. At this date still in red and cream, it would be painted green and cream in July 1972, shortly before the introduction of NBC's corporate image.** Chris Warren

Left: **The illuminated offside advertisement shows well in this view of Bristol FSF6B 2036 (WNJ 36), on route 1 to Whitehawk on 23 November 1969. Formerly BH&D 36, this vehicle, along with three others of its type, would be sold in October 1974 for further service with Hants & Dorset Motor Services.** Chris Warren

Above: **Ordered by BH&D, a batch of 10 ECW-bodied Bristol VRs were delivered direct to Southdown in the spring of 1969, becoming the company's first rear-engined double-deckers. Perpetuating BH&D's red and cream livery, they entered service with their intended fleet numbers but with Southdown-style 'CD' registrations. Seen on 25 May 1969 in Kingsway, Hove, 95 (OCD 765G) would be renumbered the following month as 2095.** Chris Warren

Above: **The Northern Counties-bodied Daimler Fleetlines of 1969-71 were handsome vehicles. Ordered for the main Southdown fleet, the first 10 — long-wheelbase dual-door versions with Gardner engines — were allocated instead to BH&D garages and thus entered service in red and cream, as demonstrated by 2108 (PUF 208H) in Church Road, Hove, on 13 October 1972. In the background can be seen the modern incarnation of Hove Town Hall rising from the ashes of a disastrous fire which destroyed the earlier building.** Chris Warren

The last BET-style saloons delivered to Southdown were a batch of 10 Marshall-bodied Bristol REs which arrived in the autumn of 1970. Short-wheelbase RESL models fitted with Leyland's powerful 680 engine, they were intended primarily for the hilly 38 route in Brighton, but 488 (TCD 488J) was photographed opposite Worthing Pier on 14 March 1971. Chris Warren

Further Bristol RESLs delivered in 1970 were a trio of dual-door ECW-bodied examples. Two, for the BH&D fleet, arrived in red and cream, but the third was delivered in Southdown green and cream as 600 (TCD 600J). However, the route for which it was intended failed to materialise, and early in 1971 it was repainted red and cream to join its sisters on BH&D work as No 2213. Coming close, in the eyes of this writer (JB), to perfection, it is seen thus in Cromwell Road, Hove, on 19 June 1971. Chris Warren

A further 15 long-wheelbase Fleetlines — again with Northern Counties bodywork but this time with Leyland engines — allocated to the BH&D fleet in 1971 turned out to be the last vehicles delivered in red and cream. Brand-new 2121 (VUF 321K) looks absolutely superb in this view at Brighton's Old Steine on 30 August 1971. Chris Warren

Above: **Four for the price of one at Brighton's Pool Valley bus station on 29 July 1972, with ECW-bodied Daimler Fleetline 386 (XUF 386K) playing the starring role. Delivered just two months previously, it was one of Southdown's final batch of Fleetlines, with Leyland engines, NBC policy thereafter favouring the Bristol VR. Alongside are sister vehicle 398 (XUF 398K), Leyland Leopard/Marshall 191 (KCD 191F) of 1967 and Leyland PD3/Northern Counties 916 (6916 CD), new in 1961.** Chris Warren

Above: **Also in 1972 Southdown took into stock 15 dual-door Bristol VRs for local services in the Brighton area. The first 10 joined the BH&D fleet, becoming the first (and, as it turned out, only) new vehicles to do so in Southdown green and cream. The other five, represented by 539 (WUF 539K) in Lower Bevendean on 15 September 1972, were allocated initially to 'pure' Southdown garages before joining their sisters in November. These were the last new vehicles delivered in traditional Southdown colours.** Chris Warren

2

THE NATIONAL IMAGE

IT WAS inevitable. It had to happen, and it did in 1972, when Frederick Wood was appointed as Chairman of the National Bus Company. A Yorkshireman by birth, Wood had spent some years in North America and came to NBC with visions of a nationwide network similar to that operated by the famous Greyhound company. His first action was to introduce a corporate livery.

A design consultant came up with a logo consisting of an italicised letter 'N' with another reflected beneath it. Depending on how you looked at it, it could also be seen as an arrowhead, and, when applied to vehicles, it always pointed in the direction of travel.

Wood's attention then turned to the question of vehicle liveries. With a few exceptions most bus companies had a basically red or green livery and thus they were offered a choice of liveries for stage-carriage vehicles: poppy red or leaf green. Some relief was provided by a white waistband (although in some early instances this was omitted) and flake-grey wheels. Fleetnames, in white, were applied in 8in-high block capitals. With the introduction of

the new image advertisements had begun to appear on the sides of double-deckers proclaiming 'We're proud to be part of the National Bus Company', which was probably far from the truth; indeed, it must have been heartbreaking for Southdown's painters to watch the superb apple green and primrose colours, with traditional fleetnames in ornate capitals or Mackenzie script, disappearing under such uninspiring tones.

Initially buses operating from former BH&D depots continued to display SOUTHDOWN-B-H&D fleetnames, albeit from 1972 in corporate style, but in 1974 the '-B-H&D' was removed, leaving an odd gap between the 'SOUTHDOWN' and double N on the offside.

In 1969 the National Bus Company had joined forces with British Leyland (now also state-owned) to produce what was hailed as the ultimate single-decker. Known as the Leyland National, the vehicle was built up from pre-fabricated parts, or modules, which allowed for a variety of lengths and door arrangements to be offered. It was originally conceived as a universal workhorse suitable for

One of the first Southdown vehicles to don corporate NBC livery, in September 1972, was Bristol RELL/ECW 603 (UCD 603J), one of a batch of three, delivered in March 1971, that proved to be the company's last REs. It is seen here at Preston Circus, Brighton, on 12 November 1972.
Chris Warren

Pending repainting in leaf green the majority of Southdown vehicles had the new-style fleetname applied to their existing livery. Having been so treated the previous year, Northern Counties-bodied Leyland Titan PD3/4 426 (BUF 426C) heads along Eastbourne seafront in open-top form in the summer of 1974. Passing an Eastbourne Corporation Leyland Panther near The Meads, it is nearing the end of its long circular trip on route 197 via East Dean, Birling Gap and Beachy Head John Bishop / Online Transport Archive

urban, suburban and even coaching work; in the event it fulfilled all of these aims, plus a few others such as ambulances and even a mobile bank!

Southdown's first Leyland Nationals, 25 in number, arrived in 1973, and, whatever their technical advances, their overall appearance did little to enhance their passenger appeal. For a start they were delivered in unrelieved leaf green, whilst internally they were fitted with hard PVC-covered seats, the side panels and seat-backs being a clinical off-white — a stark contrast to Southdown's traditional plush interiors. Nevertheless,

as elsewhere the National was to be the standard single-decker of the 'Seventies, and the clatter of the 510 fixed-head engine — frequently accompanied by clouds of black smoke — would become a familiar sound throughout the company's area.

The Bristol VR was firmly established as the standard double-decker, but in 1974 something of a stir was caused by the inclusion in the NBC's order for 174 Leyland Atlantean AN68s with Park Royal bodywork. No fewer than 41 of these were delivered to Southdown, a further six following in 1975.

Southdown's first Leyland Nationals arrived in February 1972 in unrelieved leaf green, which came as something of a shock to those used to traditional Southdown livery. Among the initial delivery was 7 (BCD 807L), seen here in the yard at the rear of Bognor Regis bus station in June 1974. Behind is a newly delivered Leyland Atlantean, one of 41 that would be received that year. John Bishop / Online Transport Archive

One consequence of Southdown's takeover of Brighton, Hove & District was the appearance on ex-BH&D routes of 'Queen Mary' Leyland PD3s, which were used to supplement and ultimately replace the native Bristol types. Among many such vehicles that would be transferred to Conway Street and Whitehawk from traditional Southdown garages was 250 (BUF 250C), seen in Church Road, Hove, on 1 October 1973. Still in apple green and cream, it has had '**SOUTHDOWN**' and '**B-H&D**' fleetnames applied in corporate NBC style.
Chris Warren / Southdown Enthusiasts' Club

The corporate '**SOUTHDOWN-B-H&D**' fleetname is shown to good advantage in this early-1970s view of Northern Counties-bodied Leyland Titan PD3/4 No 262 (BUF 262C) at the top of Elm Grove, Brighton, on route 2A. Note that the destination screen has been blanked off to show only the ultimate destination.
Glyn Kraemer-Johnson collection

In the Brighton area the early 1970s brought enormous changes in terms of services, vehicles and liveries. At the Shoreham Beach terminus of route 2, where traditionalists would have expected a red and cream Bristol, was to be found on 22 September 1973 another of the 1965 batch of Leyland PD3s, still in green and cream. No 267 (BUF 267C) stands serenely in the autumn sunshine before commencing the long trek back to Rottingdean.
Chris Warren / Southdown Enthusiasts' Club

Above: **Despite the spread of one-man operation (as it was then known) the 'Queen Mary' PD3s remained in use on some important trunk routes, notably the 230 between Brighton and Worthing. Based at the latter was an unusual specimen, 257 (BUF 257C), one of two fitted with an experimental heating and cooling system (note the lack of a radiator cap at the front), seen here in Brighton's Pool Valley bus station. Just visible on the left of the picture is an Isetta bubble car, possibly manufactured at the old Brighton railway works.** John Bishop / Online Transport Archive

Above: **An early repaint into NBC leaf green, Leyland PD3/Northern Counties 287 (FCD 287D) was yet another of its type to be cascaded in the early 1970s to ex-BH&D routes in Brighton and Hove, being seen opposite The Grenadier, Hangleton, on 24 February 1974.** Chris Warren / Southdown Enthusiasts' Club

Right: **Seen in open-top form on seafront route 17, Bristol LDS6B/ECW 2001 (OPN 801) leaves Rottingdean for Hove lagoon with a good load. BH&D's first Lodekka, appropriately numbered 1, it had been new in 1959 as one of an initial trio of convertible open-toppers painted cream for use on this service. All three succumbed to a coat of NBC leaf green in May 1974.** Southdown Enthusiasts' Club

Left: **For a period of about a year, between September 1971 and the introduction of NBC's corporate image in September 1972, ex-BH&D vehicles were repainted in traditional Southdown colours. The last of these was Bristol FS6B 2021 (SPM 21), seen on 16 February 1974 in Ham Road, Shoreham-by-Sea, on long-established route 2. Although it has by now gained NBC-style fleetnames it would never succumb to leaf green, even being repainted in traditional colours in August 1977, thereby ensuring that the bus fleet was never 100% leaf green.** Chris Warren / Southdown Enthusiasts' Club

Right: **Contrasting with sister 2021 in the previous picture, Bristol FS6B/ECW 2022 (SPM 22), photographed inside Portslade Works in May 1974, has just received a coat of NBC leaf green. Note the roof-mounted fleet number applied to convertible open-toppers. In the background can be seen ECW-bodied Leyland Tiger PS1 D691 (GUF 729), which had served latterly as a left-luggage office.** Southdown Enthusiasts' Club

Right: **The majority of the FSF-type Lodekkas were repainted in green and cream in 1971/2. Bristol-engined 2029 (UAP 29), new in 1961 as BH&D 29, is seen at Churchill Square, Brighton, on 19 August 1973. Note, above the entrance, the nearside route-number aperture, now out of use; also the grey wheels, which, together with the fleetname, indicate increasing NBC influence.** Chris Warren / Southdown Enthusiasts' Club

Below: **Five of the FSF Lodekkas were fitted with Gardner 6LW engines, among them 2031 (VAP 31), delivered in 1961 and seen** c**1974 at the Mackie Avenue, Patcham, terminus of route 5, with NBC-style fleetnames added to Southdown green and cream livery.** Southdown Enthusiasts' Club

Above: **One of the most ambitious tours organised by the Southdown Enthusiasts' Club was that undertaken on 30 September 1973 to Lille, in northern France, using ex-BH&D Bristol FS6G 2045 (XPM 45). Here seen waiting to board the ferry at Dover, it is still in red and cream with traditional BH&D fleetnames, the only evidence of NBC ownership being the grey wheels.** John Bishop / Online Transport Archive

Above: **Aside from a pair of convertible open-toppers the FS-type Lodekkas of 1964/5 all gained traditional Southdown green and cream in 1971/2. The last to remain in service in these colours was 2065 (DPM 65C), here showing off the type's classic lines from a different angle at Churchill Square, Brighton, on 29 April 1977. By this time the '-B-H&D' suffix had been removed from the fleetname, wiping out all reference to the vehicle's original owner.** Paul Gainsbury / Southdown Enthusiasts' Club

Among the first ex-BH&D vehicles in leaf green were the FLF-type Lodekkas of 1965/6, which were due for their mid-life repaint when NBC's corporate image was introduced. Outshopped in the autumn of 1972, 2074 (FPM 74C) passes through Brighton's Old Steine on coastal route 55 to East Saltdean. *Southdown Enthusiasts' Club*

A brace of Bristol Lodekkas at Brighton's Race Hill in the early 1970s provide a comparison of Southdown liveries. On the left, in NBC leaf green, is Bristol FLF6G 2079 (HPN 79D) of 1966, while on the right is similar 2075 (FPM 75C), new the previous year and one of only two of its type to wear traditional green and cream. *Southdown Enthusiasts' Club*

Left: **Early in 1974 the decision was taken to dispense with the '-B-H&D'** fleetname suffix on vehicles based at Conway Street and Whitehawk depots. Passing characteristic Sussex flint-stone walling at the top of Bear Road, Brighton, in the mid-1970s, Leyland PD3/Northern Counties 250 (BUF 250C) is seen on the extended route 6 to Woodingdean. Southdown Enthusiasts' Club

Below: **In the autumn of 1970 Southdown had taken delivery of 15 Northern Counties-bodied Daimler Fleetlines similar to the initial 10 for the BH&D fleet but with single-door layout and a shorter wheelbase. Bound for Shoreham-by-Sea on 6 April 1974, 373 (TCD 373J)** passes over the old railway bridge at Bramber on route 80, introduced as a replacement route for the Horsham–Shoreham railway service. Chris Warren

Above: **Adorned with advertising for local department store Jordan & Cook, ECW-bodied Daimler Fleetline 398 (XUF 398K)** looks every inch a Worthing vehicle as it heads along the town's seafront on 27 May 1974, by which time it had gained NBC-style fleetnames. Behind can be seen Leyland PD3/5 915 (6915 CD) in a livery publicising Roberts Off-Licences; painted thus in December 1971, it had been NBC's first example of this type of advertisement.
Chris Warren

Right: **By the end of 1975 the 15 ECW-bodied Fleetlines of 1972 had all been repainted in NBC leaf green. Outshopped thus in April, 390 (XUF 390K)** is seen in Basin Road, Chichester on 26 July 1975. By this time the majority of these vehicles had settled at garages in West Sussex.
Chris Warren

The last vehicles delivered in BH&D red and cream — 15 Leyland-engined Fleetlines new in the late summer of 1971 — retained these colours until the latter half of 1974. Looking a little uncomfortable with NBC-style fleetnames, 2113 (VUF 313K) was photographed c1973 at Brighton's Old Steine. Southdown Enthusiasts' Club

The last new vehicles for BH&D prior to the Southdown takeover had been 10 fine-looking ECW-bodied Bristol RESLs delivered in the summer of 1968.
New as BH&D 204, 2204 (PPM 204G) was still in red and cream — albeit looking incongruous with NBC-style **'SOUTHDOWN'** fleetname — when photographed in Brighton's Bristol Estate in 1974. Southdown Enthusiasts' Club

With the repaint of sister 2204 (seen above) Bristol RESL/ECW 2206 (PPM 206G) became the last bus to retain BH&D red and cream. On 18 January 1975 it was hired by the Southdown Enthusiasts' Club for a tour of traditional BH&D routes, being seen here in Portslade Old Village re-enacting a long-withdrawn route to Mile Oak. The inevitable repaint in leaf green followed in **March**. John Bishop / Online Transport Archive

By the end of 1974 all buses had NBC logos and fleetnames, including this pair of ex-BH&D Bristol KSWs relegated to driver-training duties and seen outside the west garage in Conway Street, Hove. T442 (GPM 902) even went so far as to claim that it was 'really going places'. Chris Warren

The following year T442 realised its aspirations, for on 7 February 1975 its new career as a driver-trainer took it as far afield as Eastbourne. This photograph shows it leaving the coach station in Cavendish Place, passing the splendid art-deco offices which, sadly, would be demolished in the summer of 2007. John Bishop / Online Transport Archive

Left: Another type to survive on driver-training work in the mid-1970s was the Park Royal-bodied Leyland PD2/12, the last examples of which had been withdrawn from normal service in 1971. Still in green and cream, T769 (OCD 769) was photographed in November 1975 in Churchdale Road, Eastbourne, with the old Eastbourne Corporation bus garage (since demolished) visible in the background. John Bishop / Online Transport Archive

Right: In 1972 the Series 1 Bristol VRs ordered by BH&D migrated west to Portsmouth, forsaking their original livery of red and cream for Southdown green and cream. Still so attired three years later, albeit with NBC-style fleetnames, 2100 (OCD 770G) was photographed at South Parade, Southsea, on 3 May 1975. Behind is a convertible Leyland Titan PD3, 411 (411 DCD), recently repainted in leaf green. Just behind the bus stop can be seen the roof of the inspector's kiosk which now resides at the Amberley Working Museum in West Sussex. Chris Warren

Below: Southdown's largest depot in the Portsmouth area was at Hilsea, on the city's northern outskirts. Seen inside the east garage is 2102 (OCD 772G), another of the BH&D VRs transferred west in 1972. Whether by accident or design, the registrations selected for these buses recalled Southdown's Park Royal-bodied Leyland PD2s of 1955, one of which is seen at the top of this page. John Bishop / Online Transport Archive

The Series 1 VRs transferred to Portsmouth were replaced in Brighton by new dual-door examples. Still in traditional green and cream, 538 (WUF 538K) is seen passing the Clock Tower *c*1975. Note also the Brighton Corporation Leyland PD2 on route 7 to Ovingdean. John Fozard

The last new vehicle delivered in Southdown's traditional livery of green and cream, in July 1972, dual-door Bristol VR 541 (WUF 541K) retained these colours when photographed *c*1975 in Brighton's Old Steine. By now the short-lived 'small gold block' fleetname had given way to the NBC corporate style; the gap between '**SOUTHDOWN**' and the double-N logo has been created by the deletion of the '**-B-H&D**' suffix. John Bishop / Online Transport Archive

Repainted in leaf green, the later 'Queen Mary' Leyland PD3s continued to provide sterling service in the mid-1970s, not least the convertible open-toppers of 1964/5. Pictured in the summer of 1974, 402 (402 DCD), adorned with appropriate promotional material has arrived at Beachy Head — '600ft above sea level' — on route 97 from Eastbourne. John Bishop / Online Transport Archive

Some relief from leaf green was provided by the 1970s craze for overall advertisements. In 1975 Leyland PD3/4 281 (BUF 281C) was outshopped in this dramatic scheme to the order of the Newhaven-based Sapphire Carpet & Furniture Warehouse. When photographed in Seaford it still retained a traditional 'Southdown' grille badge and a gold fleet number below the offside headlights. John Bishop / Online Transport Archive

The 230 Brighton–Worthing route remained a 'Queen Mary' stronghold throughout the 1970s. Pictured on Worthing seafront c1976 is 277 (BUF 277C), its re-panelled front (minus the chrome grille surround) rendering it somewhat plain in appearance. Jostling for position behind are a dual-purpose Leyland Leopard and a Daimler Fleetline — both, like the PD3, bodied by Northern Counties. John Bishop / Online Transport Archive

Another 'Queen Mary' treated to overall advertising was 263 (BUF 263C), which from February 1973 promoted Rediffusion colour televisions. This photograph, taken in April 1975, shows it parked in the yard behind Bognor Regis bus station.
John Bishop / Online Transport Archive

Right: **The oldest single-deckers repainted in leaf green were BET-style Marshall-bodied Leyland Leopards dating from 1963. Thus attired but already 'patched up', 116 (116 CUF) was photographed in April 1975 at Prince's Park, Eastbourne, near the Southdown garage in Royal Parade. Route 97 was normally the preserve of open-top double-deckers requiring the services of a conductor. In the background (right) is the site of the Eastbourne Miniature Tramway, closed in 1969.** John Bishop / Online Transport Archive

Below right: **Another Eastbourne view from April 1975, this time recorded at the town's Pevensey Road bus station and featuring BET-style Leopard/ Weymann 147 (EUF 147D). Delivered in 1966, this was one of 20 such vehicles which in terms of styling were virtually indistinguishable from the more numerous Marshall-bodied examples. Again, the supposedly leaf-green paintwork has been patched, to the extent that the bus appears to be wearing at least three different shades!** John Bishop / Online Transport Archive

Below: **Resting between duties in June 1974, Leopard/Marshall 164 (HUF 764E) of 1967 stands alongside a London Country RT in Brighton's Pool Valley bus station. This batch was identifiable by the decorative aluminium strip across the lower front, intended to look like a bumper, although 164 has by now lost the two outer sections.** John Bishop / Online Transport Archive

Left: **A good load of passengers seems to be enjoying the fine weather and beautiful West Sussex countryside near Henfield as another of the 1967 Leopard/Marshalls, 193 (KCD 193F), makes its way from Horsham to Brighton** c1975. **Many of this batch (although not 193) would later have the distinctive V-shaped front beading modified to facilitate continuation of the white waistband around the front of the vehicle.**
Southdown Enthusiasts' Club

Left: **The third builder to supply Southdown with saloon bodywork to BET Federation style was Willowbrook, its products distinguishable through lacking the 'V'-shaped beading at the front. One of a batch of 15 Leopards delivered early in 1968, 206 (KUF 206F) is seen** c1973 **in Lewes bus station** en route **from Brighton to Ringmer. Note that, curiously, initial repaints into NBC livery did not take advantage of the revised frontal mouldings, the white waistband stopping aft of the cab window.**
Southdown Enthusiasts' Club

Below: **Something of an odd man out was Southdown Leyland Leopard 480 (EUF 224D), the chassis of which had started life as the basis of a Plaxton-bodied coach (1224) delivered in 1966. Following accident damage it was sent to Willowbrook for rebodying to the contemporary BET Federation bus style, returning thus in December 1968, renumbered to follow on from the batch of Northern Counties-bodied Leopards then on order. In appearance it was very similar to the 15 Leopard/Willowbrooks delivered earlier in the year, as apparent from this 1973 photograph, which shows it at Brighton's Old Steine in company with a 'Queen Mary' Leyland PD3 in traditional Southdown green and cream and a Daimler Fleetline in BH&D red and cream.** John Bishop / Online Transport Archive

Numerically the last of 30 dual-purpose Northern Counties-bodied Leyland Leopards delivered in 1969, 479 (PUF 179H) was one of the first Southdown vehicles to be repainted in leaf green, in September 1972. Surprisingly, however, it was outshopped in bus-style livery of green with white waistband, being seen thus at Horsham depot. *Southdown Enthusiasts' Club*

Subsequent repaints of the Northern Counties-bodied Leopards were in green and white 'local coach' livery befitting their dual-purpose status. Representing this style on Worthing seafront in the summer of 1976 is an immaculate 472 (PUF 172H), collecting passengers for Findon on local service 205. *John Bishop / Online Transport Archive*

The trio of ECW-bodied Bristol RELLs delivered in March 1971 spent their early lives in the Brighton area, generally on local services to West Dene. However, 601 (UCD 601J) is seen here at the unlikely location of Maidstone bus station, where it had paused on 29 June 1975 whilst on a Southdown Enthusiasts' Club tour to Kent. John Bishop / Online Transport Archive

Representing the new order in terms of single-deck deliveries in May 1974 is Leyland National 19 (BCD 819L), delivered a year previously and seen in the Old Steine, Brighton, on long-established route 9 to Arundel. In the background can be seen a pair of Brighton Corporation Willowbrook-bodied Leyland Atlanteans of similar vintage. John Bishop / Online Transport Archive

Left: The only vehicles delivered new with 'SOUTHDOWN-B-H&D' fleetnames in NBC corporate style were a batch of 14 single-door Bristol VRs that arrived in 1973/4. Still devoid of advertisements, 557 (NCD 557M) had not long been in service when photographed near Brighton's Royal Pavilion. Behind are a Brighton Corporation Leyland PD3 and an ex-BH&D Bristol FSF, whilst on the right a Southdown BET-style Leyland Leopard can be seen inching its way out of Edward Street garage, destined to close in 1981 and soon afterwards demolished for redevelopment. John Bishop / Online Transport Archive

Left: Overall advertisements were not confined to the 'Queen Marys'; in August 1972 Bristol VR 505 (SCD 505H) of 1970 received this garish scheme to the order of Zetter's Pools, being depicted thus on a wet 6 May 1973 at the Old Steine, Brighton. Photo Five Transport Enterprises

Below: The last of the 1973/4 batch of VRs, 563 (NCD 563M), was also the last vehicle delivered with 'SOUTHDOWN-B-H&D' fleetnames, though these were removed before it entered service in May. In November of the same year it joined the growing band of double-deckers treated to overall advertising, in this case for Old Holborn tobacco. It was photographed thus in April 1975 while on layover in Brighton's Old Steine. Just visible in the background is a Corporation Atlantean/Willowbrook promoting Tesco. John Bishop / Online Transport Archive

Portsmouth also had its share of overall advertisements. This mid-1970s scene at Southsea features VR 518 (UUF 118J) of 1971, repainted in March 1974 in this vivid scheme to promote the Solid Fuel Advisory Service. Behind can be seen one of the then new Leyland Atlanteans and 'Queen Mary' 270 (BUF 270C) in yet another advertising livery, for London & Manchester Assurance. John Bishop / Online Transport Archive

Having eschewed the type in BET days, Southdown took delivery of its first Leyland Atlanteans, with Park Royal bodywork finished by Roe, in the spring of 1974. On 16 June the Southdown Enthusiasts' Club took brand-new 720 (PUF 720M) to the popular Southsea Spectacular rally, where it is seen posed next to the company-owned preserved Leyland G7 0145 (CD 7045) of 1922. John Bishop / Online Transport Archive

3
FEWER STOPS, MORE SWAPS

IN THE mid-'Seventies was hatched one of the more successful ideas of the NBC era: the introduction of limited-stop services. Most were numbered in the 7xx series, possibly emulating London Transport's Green Line services. First to hit the road, in January 1975, was a limited-stop version of Southdown's long-established 31 route between Brighton and Portsmouth. Numbered 700 and branded 'Coastliner', it was worked by the new Atlanteans, suitably adorned with full-length posters advertising the service. The second batch of Atlanteans, along with a pair of Bristol VRs, were used from March 1976 on a new service (X71) between Portsmouth and Southampton. Branded 'Solenteer', this was operated jointly with Hants & Dorset.

A third limited-stop service was the 729 'Regency Route' between Brighton and Tunbridge Wells. Introduced in January 1977 and operated jointly with Maidstone & District, this replaced the old 119 service, while at the same time the lengthy 122 from Brighton to Gravesend was cut back to run between Gravesend and Tunbridge Wells and became operated solely by Maidstone & District. Another long-established service to be given the limited-stop

treatment, at least in the Brighton area, was the 12 (now renumbered 112 and later to become the 712) between Brighton and Eastbourne.

In Brighton itself a network of 'Timesaver' services was introduced, these running mainly at peak-times between the outlying areas and the town centre and, in the main, shadowing the normal stopping services. The idea was probably a good one, but the timing was wrong. The Transport Act that had created the National Bus Company had also demanded a reduction in the permitted hours for drivers, which, in turn, had created staffing problems for a number of companies, Southdown included. The new legislation meant that duties normally carried out by staff on overtime or rest-day working were no longer covered, resulting in the cancellation of many services. Every morning long lists of cancellations would be read out on local radio, and, as they were covered by other services, the Timesaver services were usually amongst the first to go. In the end they simply fizzled out.

At one point staff and vehicle shortages in the Brighton area were so severe that buses and crews from Worthing depot were drafted in at weekends to cover crew-operated

One of the two Ford/Alexander S-type midibuses delivered in 1976, 651 (LWV 651P) is seen working a rural route in the Horsham area. Photographs of the pair are something of a rarity, for in the spring of 1977 both were transferred to **Western National.** D. Clark / Southdown Enthusiasts' Club

Within a few months of delivery the six Leyland Atlanteans received in December 1975 — all based at Portsmouth — were given branding for the limited-stop 'Solenteer' service (X71) between Portsmouth and Southampton, introduced on 7 March 1976. However, in this busy scene, recorded at Bognor Regis in April 1978, 745 (LCD 45P) has escaped to the 700 'Coastliner', introduced in January 1975 to replace the well-known 31 between Portsmouth and Brighton.
John Bishop / Online Transport Archive

services 1, 2 and 5, resulting in some unusual vehicle types appearing on these services including Leopards, REs and short Fleetlines. It was a time when almost anything that moved would be pressed into service, and on more than one occasion I travelled home to Patcham on a Ford coach in National white livery and with a full standing load, the conductor valiantly trying to battle his way down the narrow gangway!

Due to the non-standard nature of its vehicles, the former Brighton, Hove & District fleet had been left virtually intact and still allocated to the original depots at Conway Street and Whitehawk. The OCD-registered VRs had migrated to Portsmouth in 1972 and were followed in 1977 by the RESLs, both types already featuring in the main Southdown fleet. The Lodekkas remained a prominent sight in the Brighton area, although a number had already begun to appear elsewhere in Southdown territory, notably in the summer of 1975 on the Hayling Island open-top service (333). Unfortunately by this time they had lost their smart cream and black livery and adopted the standard leaf green with white band, unlike similar vehicles operated by other NBC subsidiaries, notably Southern Vectis, which company's open-toppers appeared in an attractive livery of white with green lower panels.

It cannot be denied that like most early rear-engined buses, the first Bristol VRs were far from trouble-free. Whereas English operators, with one or two exceptions, made the best of a bad job, the Scottish Bus Group was adamant in its dislike of the type — so much so that agreement was eventually reached between the NBC and SBG whereby some 91 VRs would come south in exchange for Bristol FLF front-engined buses. Southdown dispatched the eight newest FLFs from the BH&D fleet and in return received an equal number of early VRs, unusual in being 83-seaters of 33ft length. They differed from the standard VR through having fewer opening windows and SBG's characteristic six-sided destination screen, which surprisingly they were to retain throughout their lives with Southdown. They were allocated to Brighton, whence had come the FLFs, but the unions objected to the operation of such high-capacity buses, and they were down-seated to 74 prior to entering service in the spring of 1973.

Unusual vehicles delivered to the fleet in 1976, apparently at the behest of NBC, were two Alexander-bodied Ford midibuses. Southdown tried them on a number of rural services, but after less than a year they were winging their way to pastures new with Western National.

The 'Queen Mary' PD3s continued in service in diminishing numbers as the 1970s wore on, most gravitating to local services in the Brighton area. Having endured the stiff climb up Freshfield Road, 278 (BUF 278C), dating from 1965, takes a well-earned rest at the Race Hill before returning to Portslade. Southdown Enthusiasts' Club

The last PD3s delivered to Southdown were the 'Panoramics' of 1967. Emerging from the bus station in Pevensey Road in April 1975, 369 (HCD 369E) is seen at the start of its journey on trunk route 112 (formerly 12) to Brighton. The bus station has long since closed, although the building still stands. John Bishop / Online Transport Archive

Looking smart at Hove's Conway Street depot following a repaint in 1977, Leyland PD3 415 (415 DCD) shows off the new-style NBC logo introduced the previous year, with the double-N device in red and blue on a white background. Although older than either of the buses depicted above, the convertible PD3s would enjoy a longer lifespan due to their versatility, being found useful as open-toppers in the summer months and for the lucrative Derby Day contracts. John Bishop / Online Transport Archive

In NBC days yellow became the standard colour for driver-training buses. Repainted thus from green and cream the previous year, Park Royal-bodied Leyland PD2/12 T765 (OCD 765) was photographed at Conway Street on 20 August 1977. By now already 22 years old, it and three similar buses would continue in this role until displaced in 1980 by 'Panoramic' PD3s of the type seen opposite. Chris Warren / Southdown Enthusiasts' Club

Also part of Southdown's driver-training fleet in the mid-1970s were the four survivors from the 1961 batch of Leyland PD3s, which were relegated to these duties in 1974/5. T877 (2877 CD) is seen in Eastbourne outside the South East Traffic Commissioner's office in Ivy Terrace, where no doubt a very nervous trainee was awaiting the result of his test! Behind can be seen an Eastbourne Borough Council Leyland PD2, also on training duties. John Bishop / Online Transport Archive

Recently repainted in leaf green, Marshall-bodied Leyland Leopard 123 (BUF 123C) of 1965 is seen c1976 in Brighton's West Dene estate. As was the case elsewhere in Southdown territory, various routes in the Brighton area were subject to renumbering in the mid-1970s, West Dene having been served hitherto by route 115. Dave Warren / Southdown Enthusiasts' Club

In the mid-1970s the majority of Southdown's inland services remained in the hands of Leyland Leopard and Bristol RE saloons with BET-style bodywork. In March 1977 at Haywards Heath bus station, Leopard/Weymann 149 (EUF 149D) has had the distinctive V-shaped beading replaced to facilitate continuation of the white waistband around the front of the vehicle (see page 26). The bus station at Haywards Heath would close c1980, although the building still stands today. John Bishop / Online Transport Archive

Basking in the sunshine at Worthing depot in September 1975 is Bristol RESL/Marshall 231 (KUF 231F), one of a batch of 40 new in 1968 with Gardner engines and manual gearboxes. Alongside are one of the following year's delivery of 20 Bristol RELLs and, unusually, an ex-BH&D Bristol FS, while on the left can be seen one of the handsome Harrington Cavalier-bodied Leyland Leopards of the early 1960s. Sadly this part of the depot, which doubled as a coach station and as such featured in the film *Wish You Were Here*, has since been demolished, although two other buildings remain. John Bishop / Online Transport Archive

Another view at Worthing, this time on the seafront opposite the depot, as Marshall-bodied Bristol RELL 437 (NUF 437G) of 1969 overtakes 1970 Daimler Fleetline/Northern Counties 381 (TCD 381J) in the summer of 1976. By this time the-single-door Fleetlines had generally settled at garages in West Sussex. John Bishop / Online Transport Archive

Fresh from overhaul, Daimler Fleetline/Northern Counties 375 (TCD 375J) positively gleams in Brighton's Pool Valley bus station in July 1977, its condition a credit to the staff at Portslade Works. The destination display suggests the vehicle has arrived from Horsham, on a route that was normally the preserve of single-deckers. John Bishop / Online Transport Archive

Above: **Representing a batch of 10 ordered by BH&D but diverted to the main Southdown fleet, being one of a pair allocated new to Haywards Heath in May 1970, Bristol VR 501 (SCD 501H) had settled in its intended home by September 1975, when this photograph was taken in Brighton's Old Steine. Its destination, however, is anyone's guess, the blind display falling well short of the company's usual standards.** John Bishop / Online Transport Archive

Left: **A Northern Counties-bodied Daimler Fleetline dating from 1970, 2108 (PUF 208H) was one of a batch of 10 diverted to BH&D in exchange for the Bristol VRs represented by 501 above. Freshly outshopped in a second coat of leaf green complete with new-style NBC logo, it is seen passing the Royal Sussex County Hospital in Eastern Road on 8 August 1976, by which time the last vestiges of red and cream had been expunged from Brighton's bus fleet.** Chris Warren

With their powerful Leyland engines the Marshall-bodied Bristol RESLs of 1970 were ideally suited to some of the less busy routes in hilly Brighton. Just how hilly is apparent from this view of recently overhauled 482 (TCD 482J) storming up Coombe Road on its way to Bevendean Hospital on 7 May 1977. Chris Warren

The Leyland-engined RESLs of 1970 also appeared on other local routes in Brighton, notably the 34/35 group of services to West Dene. No 482 is seen again the following month in Pool Valley bus station. Happily 481 of this batch survives in preservation in traditional green and cream livery. John Bishop / Online Transport Archive

The ECW-bodied RESLs remained in Brighton for much of the 1970s. Repainted in leaf green, they never looked as good as when in red and cream but were still handsome vehicles, as apparent from this view of 2212 (TCD 612J) in Lower Bevendean on 3 April 1976. Note the gap where '-B-H&D' has been deleted from the fleetname. Chris Warren

Above: **An unusual development for Southdown was the acquisition in 1973 of second-hand vehicles, in the shape of eight Bristol VRTLLs received in February and March from Scottish Omnibuses in exchange for ex-BH&D Bristol FLF Lodekkas. Dating from 1968, 544 (LFS 296F) is seen in April 1975 at the Black Rock terminus of one-time BH&D trolleybus route 44.**
John Bishop / Online Transport Archive

Above: **Their extra length aside, the Bristol VRTLLs would always be easily recognisable by the unusually shaped destination display favoured by the Scottish Bus Group, which feature remained unmodified throughout their time at Southdown. This late-1970s photograph depicts 547 (LFS 299F) opposite the Churchill Square shopping complex in Western Road, Brighton.** Gerald Mead

Above: **Recorded outside the west garage in Conway Street, Hove, in the mid-1970s, this nearside view of 527 (WUF 527K) shows to good advantage the dual-door layout of the 1972 Bristol VRs. This example was the first to appear in leaf green, others of the batch being among the last Southdown buses to forsake the company's traditional colours.**
John Bishop / Online Transport Archive

Above: **In May 1976 Bristol VR 538 (WUF 538K), one of the dual-door batch of 1972, was given this distinctive livery to publicise the Brighton Area Travelcard, admissible not only on Southdown's buses but also on those of Brighton Corporation, as well as the local rail network. The lower half of the bus was BR Rail blue topped by a yellow waistband, the area between the decks being white; only the roof and upper-deck window surrounds were leaf green. This photograph, taken on 26 June 1976 opposite the Grenadier Hotel at Hangleton, reveals just how much cheaper were the fares of 30 years ago.** Chris Warren

Left: **The Atlanteans dedicated to the X71 'Solenteer' between Portsmouth and Southampton were assisted by a pair of Bristol VRs dating from 1974. However, in this late-1970s view 569 (GNJ 569N) has strayed to the stopping service linking Portsmouth and Fareham, being seen at the latter terminus.** Southdown Enthusiasts' Club

Below: **When new the Leyland Atlanteans of 1974 were used primarily on the company's principal trunk routes, notably the 700 Brighton–Portsmouth 'Coastliner' service, launched in January 1975, but when not so employed they appeared on secondary routes. Here 736 (SCD 736N) shows off its handsome lines at Littlehampton before returning to Worthing in April 1978.** John Bishop / Online Transport Archive

Above: **Among the limited-stop trunk routes introduced in the mid-1970s was the 729 linking Brighton and Tunbridge Wells, which, on account of the two town's royal connections, was branded the 'Regency Route'. Suitably adorned, 576 (GNJ 576N), a Bristol VR new in January 1975, is seen parked at Uckfield in June 1977. Thirty years later the Brighton & Hove Bus and Coach Company would revive the 'Regency Route' brand for an enhanced service on this route.**
John Bishop / Online Transport Archive

Above: **Early in 1977 three Southdown buses were repainted to mark the Silver Jubilee of HM The Queen, these comprising a Brighton-based Atlantean and two Bristol VRs at Portsmouth. One of the latter's contribution, 565 (GNJ 565N), is seen later that year passing the company's main garage at Hilsea.** Southdown Enthusiasts' Club

In the mid-1970s, having forsaken their original livery of overall cream for (in most cases) NBC leaf green, the convertible-open-top Bristol FS Lodekkas inherited from BH&D began to spread their wings beyond the Brighton and Hove area. One of four Gardner-engined examples delivered in 1962, 2044 (XPM 44) is seen leaving Conway Street garage to take up duty on route 277 from Brighton to Arundel.
Southdown Enthusiasts' Club

Another convertible FS6G from the same batch, 2041 (XPM 41) waits to depart Pool Valley on a Brighton local service on 18 May 1977. This was also an unusual working for an ex-BH&D vehicle, route 13 generally being the preserve of the 'pure' Southdown garages at Edward Street and Moulsecoomb. Destined to be sold in March 1978, this vehicle would see further service as a permanent open-topper with Lincolnshire Road Car.
Paul Gainsbury/ Southdown Enthusiasts' Club

A standard Bristol FS6G new to BH&D in 1963, 2055 (4655 AP) is seen on layover in Brighton's Old Steine in June 1976, the gap between fleetname and NBC logo (created by deletion of the '**-B-H&D**' suffix) revealing that this bus had been an early repaint in leaf green. Open-toppers aside, the last FS-type Lodekkas would be withdrawn and sold the following year. *John Bishop / Online Transport Archive*

Of the 20 FLF-type Lodekkas inherited from BH&D, the eight most recent examples passed in 1973 to Scottish Omnibuses in exchange for the Bristol VRTLLs (see page 40). The newest to remain in Brighton was 2084 (KPM 84E), seen c1977 in Carden Avenue, Patcham, on 'Timesaver' limited-stop service 776, which, unlike most such routes, operated throughout the day. Gerry Cork / Southdown Enthusiasts' Club

Another convertible FS-type Lodekka to venture from its traditional haunts was Bristol-engined 2051 (AAP 51B), which spent the summer of 1975 based at Hayling Island for use on open-top service 333. This photograph, taken on 26 July, shows it on layover in Sandy Point Road, Eastoke. Note the minimalist bus stops, the flags being attached to concrete lamp-posts. Chris Warren

Having escaped even further west, Bristol LDS6B 2001 (OPN 801) is seen on 21 September 1975 in the unlikely location of Bournemouth bus station whilst on loan to Hants & Dorset Motor Services. Alongside is the former 2047 (XPM 47), an FS6B sold by Southdown the previous year and now running as Hants & Dorset 3495 in NBC poppy red — a shade that would most probably have been adopted in the 1970s for buses in Brighton, had not BH&D already been merged with Southdown. John Bishop / Online Transport Archive

4
ANY EXCUSE ...

OTWITHSTANDING the strictures of NBC's corporate image, Southdown seemed glad of any excuse to revive its traditional livery; and why not? This even extended to two Ford Transit minibuses purchased for the Cuckmere Community Bus scheme, a joint venture between NBC and East Sussex County Council and serving the villages of the Cuckmere Valley. Its vehicles were driven by volunteers but maintained by Southdown, hence the full apple-green and cream livery, complete with dark green relief.

Another innovation of the NBC era was the introduction of 'open days' at Portslade Works. Star of the 1978 event was one of the ECW-bodied Daimler Fleetlines with the rear half painted in NBC leaf green and white, the front half resplendent in traditional Southdown green and cream.

A less happy event that occurred in April of the same year was a disastrous fire that swept through the ex-Brighton Hove & District garage at Conway Street, Hove, destroying 14 buses and damaging a further three. To cover the shortfall the company's last eight Bristol Lodekkas (all convertible-open-top FS types), all of which had been withdrawn for disposal, were reinstated and immediately pressed into service. Thus reprieved, four of them, including two that had managed to retain Southdown green and cream, would survive long enough to be transferred to the reactivated Brighton, Hove & District company in 1986.

During the late 'Seventies and early 'Eighties a number of NBC subsidiaries took part in the Market Analysis Project (MAP), in which surveys were carried out to ascertain the habits and requirements of the travelling public, services

being amended accordingly. In many parts of the country this manifested itself in the introduction of local identities and fleetnames. This didn't happen in the Southdown area other than at Horsham, where buses on local services had their NBC-style fleetnames replaced by vinyl stickers proclaiming 'SOUTHDOWN' in traditional gold-block letters on a transparent background. A nice touch, but one that looked rather odd when viewed against the NBC leaf-green panels.

Deliveries of new vehicles continued apace in the late 'Seventies. Among the large numbers of Bristol VRs — many of dual-door layout, for use on local services in the Brighton and Portsmouth areas — were 30 convertible open-toppers; received in 1977/8, these were intended to replace the remaining convertible Lodekkas and Leyland PD3s (and would have done so had it not been for the Conway Street fire, which actually claimed one of these VRs among its victims). Ten of the VRs were particularly unusual through combining an open-top capability with the dual-door layout. VRs continued to arrive until 1981, the last being delivered in April of that year. Unlike most NBC subsidiaries Southdown did not receive any examples of the replacement Leyland Olympian, and, indeed, no further new double-deckers would be purchased by Southdown in the NBC era.

The Leyland National remained the standard single-decker, although the 1977/8 batches were of dual-door layout, being intended mostly for local services in Brighton or Portsmouth. In 1980 the original model was replaced by the National 2. A considerably improved vehicle, with the more powerful Leyland 680 engine, this was easily recognisable by its front-mounted radiator, which necessitated a slightly bulbous front dash.

In the early 1980s Southdown introduced further limited-stop services. The first of these was the 770, running between Brighton and Haywards Heath and branded (somewhat ironically, in view of what was to follow) as the 'Stage Coach' 770. The brand name would later spread to the aforementioned trunk routes 700 and 729, as well as the 702 (Southsea–Portsmouth–Hayling Island), 712 (Brighton–Eastbourne), 727 (Portsmouth–Southampton non-stop, operated jointly with Hampshire Bus), 728 (Brighton–Lewes), 737 (Portsmouth–Windsor), 780 (Eastbourne–East Grinstead) and 799 (Brighton–Rye, operated jointly with Hastings & District, and for a time extended westwards to Worthing).

In 1983 East Sussex County Council introduced its 'County Rider' services combining rural bus operation with the carriage of the disabled, and for this scheme Southdown acquired four Leyland Cubs with Reeve-Burgess bodies fitted with wheelchair lifts, an unlikely combination for the company but one that proved quite successful.

Undaunted by its experience with the 'Timesaver' services, Southdown now had another, ultimately more successful attempt at running limited-stop services in Brighton with the introduction in 1983 of 'Shuttle' service 60 to Mile Oak. This was worked by eight Bristol VRs in a striking livery of white front with diagonal stripes graduating from pale yellow to deep orange at the rear — a scheme shared by six Leyland National 2s used by Brighton Borough Transport on a similar service (50) to Hollingdean.

Left: **The most dramatic event to affect Southdown in the late 1970s was probably the fire which, in the early hours of 14 April 1978, swept through the west garage at Conway Street, Hove. Fortunately no lives were lost, but the cost in terms of vehicles was high, 14 being damaged beyond economic repair. This photograph, showing the charred remains of a Daimler Fleetline (2117) and a pair of 'Queen Mary' Leyland PD3s (301 and 348) as well as a gaping hole in the garage roof, gives some idea of the devastation. The building was subsequently repaired and is still used today by the Brighton & Hove Bus and Coach Co.** John Bishop / Online Transport Archive

Right: **It is said that every cloud has a silver lining, and one result of the Conway Street fire was the reinstatement of eight Bristol Lodekkas that had been withdrawn for disposal. Parked at the rear of Conway Street's east garage in May 1978 is FS6B 2021 (SPM 21), one of two such vehicles that retained traditional Southdown colours, albeit with NBC-style fleetnames and the seemingly inevitable grey wheels. Subsequently renumbered 3228 (in a series for vehicles that were regarded as fully depreciated), it would survive in this guise to pass to the revived BH&D in 1986.** John Bishop / Online Transport Archive

Above: **Displaced by new deliveries and by the more numerous Leyland PD3s, the last FLF-type Lodekkas were withdrawn in the early months of 1978. To mark their passing, on 24 January the Southdown Enthusiasts' Club hired 2076 (GPN 76D) for a farewell tour which ran as far afield as Hassocks, where this photograph was taken. Along with eight others of its type this vehicle would see further service with Alder Valley.** John Bishop / Online Transport Archive

Above right: **Another consequence of the Conway Street fire was the appearance on Brighton-area services of vehicles loaned from other garages. Pictured opposite the Grenadier Hotel in Hangleton, Hove, on 22 April 1978, Worthing's 373 (TCD 373J), a Northern Counties-bodied Daimler Fleetline dating from 1970, helps out on busy cross-town route 5.** Chris Warren

Right: **By the late 1970s the ECW-bodied Fleetlines of 1972 were all based at garages in West Sussex, being particularly associated with Chichester and Bognor Regis. One of the latter's allocation, 394 (XUF 394K), was photographed in the yard at its home depot in April 1978, by which time it was in need of a second repaint.** John Bishop / Online Transport Archive

Above: **Resplendent in a fresh coat of leaf green in April 1979, having been overhauled a few months previously, Daimler Fleetline/ECW 390 (XUF 390K) pauses on the seafront at its then home town of Worthing to collect passengers on what appears to be a short working of the Horsham service.** John Bishop / Online Transport Archive

Left: **Toward the end of their time with Southdown a number of the ECW-bodied Fleetlines appeared on local services in Brighton. Recently transferred from Chichester, 393 (XUF 393K) is seen at the Race Hill on 16 May 1980. In the autumn of that year the 30 single-door Fleetlines would be transferred *en masse* to Crosville Motor Services.** Paul Gainsbury / Southdown Enthusiasts' Club

Left: **By the late 1970s the only Leyland PD3s with a reasonable life expectancy were the convertibles of 1964/5. In 1978 these were renumbered into a new series reserved for fully depreciated vehicles (FDVs). Formerly 412, 3212 (412 DCD), was photographed on 22 September 1979 heading along the Lewes Road on Brighton local route 25 from Sussex University, although the destination display suggests more ambitious intentions!** Gerald Mead

Below left: **Repainted and renumbered, its appearance marred only by a fragmented fleetname, 3221 (422 DCD) basks in early-summer sunshine at Haywards Heath bus station in June 1979. This view shows well the squarer profile and thick beading (below the upper-deck windows) that distinguished the convertible PD3s. This example's non-matching fleet number arose from the fact that sister vehicle 421 had been demoted to a tree-lopper in 1977 following roof damage and so was not included in the following year's renumbering.** John Bishop / Online Transport Archive

Below left: **When not required as open-toppers the convertible PD3s were used on school contracts, 3223 (424 DCD) being seen thus employed in the Chichester area c1980. The somewhat piratical appearance of these vehicles in closed-top form is explained by the fact that, early in their lives, the opening part of the offside front window on the upper deck was purloined to provide extra ventilation on the 'Panoramics' of 1967. No 3223 has seemingly suffered the further misfortune of accident damage, judging by the incongruous reflective front numberplate and the lack of a chrome surround to the radiator grille.** Southdown Enthusiasts' Club

Early in 1982 convertible PD3 No 3209 was given this distinctive livery to publicise Maritime England Year, being seen in open-top form on Madeira Drive at the conclusion of the Historic Commercial Vehicle Club's London–Brighton run in May. Note the ingenious use of a dummy rear wheel disc to act as a rotating paddle-wheel; also that of the blinds to display 'MV SOUTHDOWN'. Sister vehicle 3202 would later be similarly repainted, while the following year 3215 was outshopped in a scheme, based on traditional Southdown livery, to promote 'Beautiful Britain'. The only example of its batch never to sacrifice its registration to a newer vehicle (see page 73), 3209 would itself later be restored to traditional colours and, officially numbered 19909 in Stagecoach's national system, remains in Southdown ownership today. John Bishop / Online Transport Archive

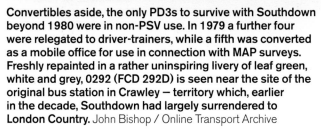

Convertibles aside, the only PD3s to survive with Southdown beyond 1980 were in non-PSV use. In 1979 a further four were relegated to driver-trainers, while a fifth was converted as a mobile office for use in connection with MAP surveys. Freshly repainted in a rather uninspiring livery of leaf green, white and grey, 0292 (FCD 292D) is seen near the site of the original bus station in Crawley — territory which, earlier in the decade, Southdown had largely surrendered to **London Country.** John Bishop / Online Transport Archive

In 1980 a final quartet of PD3s – this time 'Panoramics' from 1967 – were converted as driver-trainers, initially retaining leaf green. By now in yellow and looking rather dishevelled, T360 (HCD 360E) is seen some years later (note the new Southdown 'S' device which from 1986 began to replace the NBC double-N) performing a reversing test outside the Bird's Eye factory on the outskirts of Eastbourne. John Bishop / Online Transport Archive

In 1977 the ECW-bodied Bristol RESLs were reallocated away from Brighton, having been replaced by new Leyland Nationals. Most would spend the remainder of their Southdown careers at Portsmouth, but 2201 (PPM 201G) – the first of the batch new to BH&D in 1968 – was one of two to settle at Haywards Heath, being photographed outside the town's Perrymount Cinema (long since demolished) on 19 May 1979. Gerald Mead

Of the RESLs transferred away from Brighton 2211 (TCD 611J) – one of the trio delivered in 1970 – stayed closer to home than most, moving just up the road to Lewes. When photographed on 30 May 1978 it was approaching the Landport Estate on town service 127. Paul Gainsbury / Southdown Enthusiasts' Club

Above: **The other two RESLs of 1970 moved initially to Portsmouth. As vacant Southsea deckchairs billow on a windy day in April 1978, a recently repainted 2213 (TCD 600J) awaits passengers for Rowlands Castle. Behind is one of the 1975 Leyland Atlanteans on the X71 'Solenteer' service to Southampton.** John Bishop / Online Transport Archive

Right: **Later in 1978 RESLs 2212/3 (TCD 612, 600J) were transferred to Bognor Regis, being seen that summer parked at the rear of the town's bus station. The ECW-bodied RESLs would all be withdrawn in 1982.** John Bishop / Online Transport Archive

The 40-strong batch of Marshall-bodied Bristol RESLs delivered to Southdown in 1968 survived largely intact until 1979. *En route* to Eastbourne, 239 (KUF 239F) was photographed in Ersham Road, Hailsham, in May of that year, having recently received a second coat of leaf green with later type of double-N logo. John Bishop / Online Transport Archive

The longer Bristol RELLs of 1969 were withdrawn *en masse* in June 1980, although a handful were subsequently reinstated, renumbered in the 31xx series reserved for fully depreciated single-deckers. No 439 (NUF 439G), however, was converted for use as a staff office and mess room at Uckfield station, where it was photographed in February 1982. John Bishop / Online Transport Archive

The dual-purpose Northern Counties-bodied Leyland Leopards of 1969 were intended to spend the summer months on express coach work, but by the late 1970s they were largely confined to stage-carriage duties. Looking attractive in NBC 'local coach' livery, 464 (PUF 164H) is seen parked behind the bus station at Bognor Regis in April 1978. John Bishop / Online Transport Archive

Like the Marshall-bodied RELL saloons delivered the same year, the dual-purpose Leopards of 1969 enjoyed short lives with Southdown. Having arrived from Uckfield, 465 (PUF 165H) is seen in Terminus Road, Eastbourne, on 18 May 1980, four months before withdrawal.
Gerald Mead

With their powerful Leyland engines the 10 Marshall-bodied Bristol RESLs of 1970 proved to be fast dependable machines ideally suited to Brighton's terrain. Heading into town on local route 11 from Lower Bevendean, 481 (TCD 481J) was photographed in the Lewes Road on 22 September 1979.
Gerald Mead

Contrasting with broadly similar machines delivered a year or two previously, the Marshall-bodied REs of 1970 mostly enjoyed long lives with Southdown. On 11 July 1984 490 (TCD 490J) passes Brighton's Churchill Square shopping centre *en route* to Southwick, its revised NBC logo celebrating the fact that in 1981 Southdown had won the initial NBC Chairman's Award for Innovation, for developing computer-generated drivers' fare charts. Coincidentally all three vehicles depicted on this page survive in preservation, although at the time of writing (January 2008) 490 is still awaiting restoration. Chris Warren / Southdown Enthusiasts' Club

In 1979 NBC management decreed that single-deckers should henceforth be outshopped from overhaul minus the white waistband. Consequently a number of Southdown's earliest Leyland Nationals, delivered in 1973, emerged from mid-life overhaul in a livery similar to that carried when new. Looking plain in overall green, 8 (BCD 808L) heads along Western Road, Brighton, on 19 August 1984. Fortunately Southdown soon chose to ignore this particular dictum, and from 1981 repaints once again featured white waistbands. Gerald Mead

After a slow start, deliveries of Leyland Nationals picked up in the latter half of the 1970s. Unusually for Southdown, the 10 single-door versions delivered in 1976/7 and allocated to depots in the Eastbourne area, had non-matching fleet/registration numbers. No 34 (PCD 80R) was photographed in May 1980 in the old Uckfield bus station, long since demolished to make way for shops and a link road to the town's by-pass. Gerald Mead

In August 1979 two of the 1976 Nationals were treated to 'unibus' advertisements promoting Langney Shopping Centre, on the outskirts of Eastbourne. This unusual view of 31 (PCD 77R), recorded there in July 1980, shows well the smaller roof pod introduced on the type in the mid-1970s. John Bishop / Online Transport Archive

In 1977 Southdown took into stock 26 dual-door Leyland Nationals, all allocated initially to depots in the Brighton area and represented here by Conway Street's 57 (UFG 57S) at the Old Steine. The Leyland Atlantean behind has just arrived from Eastbourne on limited-stop service 112.
Glyn Kraemer-Johnson collection

A further 26 dual-door Nationals were delivered in 1978, the majority shared between Portsmouth and various 'country' depots in Sussex. Haywards Heath's 74 (YCD 74T) is seen in Crawley town centre on 18 August 1981. Gerald Mead

In 1980 Southdown used the introduction of MAP revisions in the Horsham area as an excuse to revive its traditional fleetname on locally allocated vehicles. One of two double-deckers so adorned was Bristol VR 2094 (OCD 764G), delivered in BH&D red and cream in the spring of 1969 and seen outside Henfield garage in the autumn of 1980. Beneath 'SOUTHDOWN' (and showing up none too well against NBC leaf green) appears the legend 'The great name behind your new services'.
John Bishop / Online Transport Archive

The single-door VRs of 1971 were generally associated with the Portsmouth area. One of two vehicles specially painted to celebrate the 50th anniversary of Portslade Works in 1978 (in this case sporting a gold vertical band amidships, intended to resemble a ribbon), 525 (WCD 525K) had long since reverted to standard livery by 15 June 1980, when this photograph was taken. In common with the majority of its batch, this vehicle would head east in the twilight of its Southdown career. Gerald Mead

By 1980 the Leyland Atlanteans, originally distributed amongst garages along the coastal strip, had gravitated to either Brighton or Portsmouth. One of the latter's contingent, 712 (PUF 142M), is seen in the city's Commercial Road on 16 June, having arrived from Waterlooville. Gerald Mead

In the autumn of 1981 Bristol VR 569 (GNJ 569N) received a livery of leaf green, white, maroon and Rail blue (carried previously by earlier VR 510) to publicise the Portsmouth Area Travelcard, the colours reflecting the fact that this could be used not only on Southdown buses but also those of the City of Portsmouth Passenger Transport Department and BR trains. *En route* for Fareham, the bus is seen with a good load at Hilsea on 17 April 1984. Calvin Churchill / Southdown Enthusiasts' Club

The late 1970s witnessed the delivery of large numbers of new Bristol VRs, including no fewer than 30 that were convertible to open-top. One of two such vehicles allocated new to Eastbourne, single-door 620 (UWV 620S) is seen in its home town on a sunny 15 May 1980 on route 499 to Bexhill and Hastings. In the summer months this vehicle and sister 621 would more usually have been employed on scenic route 197 to Beachy Head.
Gerald Mead

Pictured in less clement conditions at Bognor Regis in May 1981 is another of the convertible VRs delivered in 1977/8, 607 (UWV 607S). Alongside are two of the previous generation of 'convertibles' — Leyland PD3s 3219 and 3203 (formerly 419 and 403) of 1964 — which the new VRs were intended to replace, although in practice these old-stagers would continue to serve the company for a further decade. Notice how Kodak film accentuates the differing shades of leaf green created by fading. John Bishop / Online Transport Archive

Above: **With the canopy of Hove station as a backdrop, a brace of dual-door Bristol VRs delivered the previous autumn — 627 and 633 (UFG 627/33S) — stand at the rear of the east garage in Conway Street, Hove, in April 1978. In the same month 14 buses were lost in a disastrous fire that also severely damaged the west garage.** John Bishop / Online Transport Archive

Left: **Delivered in the summer of 1977, 10 of Southdown's convertible VRs had dual-door bodywork — a unique combination — and were allocated to the ex-BH&D garages at Conway Street and Whitehawk. Proudly displaying the Chairman's Award logo, 602 (TPN 102S) heads along Western Road, Brighton, on 19 August 1984. Sister vehicle 597 had a much shorter life, being destroyed in the Conway Street fire of April 1978 when barely six months old.** Gerald Mead

Left: **A further delivery of single-door VRs in the summer and autumn of 1978 largely displaced the Leyland Atlanteans from front-line trunk services such as the 700 'Coastliner' and X71. Seen on the latter, formerly marketed as the 'Solenteer', 643 (XAP 643S) heads into Portsmouth on 15 June 1980.** Gerald Mead

Above: **The 1979 batch of Leyland Nationals reverted to single-door layout and featured such luxuries as moquette (in lieu of vinyl) seating and overhead luggage racks. They were also the first (and, as it turned out, only) Nationals to be delivered with white waistbands, this feature having hitherto been added by Southdown. Presumably on loan to the Eastbourne area, Brighton-allocated 106 (AYJ 106T) is seen at the unlikely location of Hailsham garage in July 1981. Alas the garage, like so many in Southdown territory, is no more, having been demolished for redevelopment.** John Bishop / Online Transport Archive

Above: **The small Southdown garage at Jarvis Brook, near Crowborough, on the north-eastern fringe of the company's territory, closed in the early 1980s. The last new vehicle to be allocated was 1979 Leyland National 112 (ENJ 912V), seen lurking inside in April 1980. The site is now occupied by a printing firm.** John Bishop / Online Transport Archive

Left: **In line with the latest NBC policy, the Leyland National 2s of 1980/1 arrived in unrelieved leaf green. Its blinds already set for the return journey, Lewes-allocated 126 (JWV 126W) arrives in Brighton on service 128 from Ringmer. In the background (right), at the bottom of St James's Street, can be seen the Southdown/National Travel office.** Dave Brown

In 1980/1 Southdown acquired second-hand from neighbouring Maidstone & District seven early Leyland Nationals (including one that had been new to Southdown in the first place!). Dating from early 1973, 143 (GKE 501L) receives mechanical attention inside Hailsham garage in March 1986. In unrelieved leaf green, it displays yet another logo in lieu of NBC's double N — this time a device marking Southdown's 70th anniversary, celebrated the previous year. John Bishop / Online Transport Archive

The County Rider network, serving remote villages in the Lewes, Seaford and Uckfield areas, was an East Sussex County Council initiative. The buses used were Leyland Cubs with angular Reeve Burgess bodywork equipped with tail-mounted wheelchair lifts to facilitate the carriage of disabled passengers. Four such vehicles were taken into stock, the first arriving in 1983 in a livery of bright green. With the South Downs just visible behind, a lightly loaded 800 (KJK 800Y) is seen near Lewes on 31 May 1984. Paul Gainsbury / Southdown Enthusiasts' Club

Delivered in 1984, the other three Cubs used on County Rider services were larger vehicles and arrived in a more dignified livery of dark green. Prior to delivery displayed at the 1984 Commercial Motor Show, 802 (B802 GFG) is seen the following year in the desolate environs of Uckfield railway station. Paul Cripps

Another joint venture with East Sussex County Council saw the introduction in February 1983 of a limited-stop service between Mile Oak and Brighton town centre, branded 'Shuttle' and using a dedicated fleet of eight Southdown Bristol VRs in a striking livery of white and various shades of orange. With the Royal Pavilion, then undergoing restoration, as a backdrop, 698 (EAP 998V) passes through the Old Steine in April 1985. Brighton Borough Transport operated six similarly liveried Leyland National 2s on route 50 to Hollingdean. Calvin Churchill / Southdown Enthusiasts' Club

The last double-deckers delivered new to Southdown in the NBC era were a batch of 18 Bristol VRs that arrived in the early months of 1981. Of seven allocated initially to former BH&D garages six later donned Shuttle livery, among them 260 (JWV 260W), seen outside its home depot in Conway Street, Hove. John Bishop / Online Transport Archive

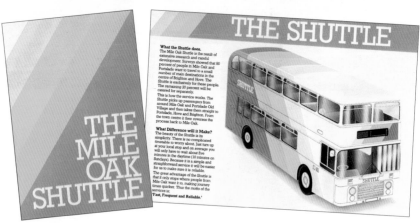

Right: The early 1980s witnessed a resurgence in overall advertising liveries on Southdown buses. One of four Bristol VRs repainted the previous autumn in a livery of red and white to promote the local *Evening Argus* newspaper, convertible 623 (UWV 623S) is seen in open-top format on Worthing seafront on 8 June 1984.
Calvin Churchill / Southdown Enthusiasts' Club

Below right: **In June 1983 Portsmouth-based VR 660 (AAP 660T), a dual-door example delivered in 1978, received a livery of red, white and blue to publicise Radio Victory, being seen heading through the city on 1 July.**
Calvin Churchill / Southdown Enthusiasts' Club

Below: **A strike at engine manufacturer L. Gardner & Sons meant that Southdown's last 11 VRs were fitted with Leyland 680 engines. One of a number of this batch subsequently adorned with promotional material for the 'Coastliner' service between Brighton and Portsmouth, 274 (JWV 274W) is seen in the former town's Pool Valley bus station.**
Southdown Enthusiasts' Club

5

A WHITER SHADE OF PALE

LITTLE mention has so far been made of the coaching fleet. NBC adopted as its standard coach chassis the Leyland Leopard, favoured by Southdown since 1961, so further deliveries of this type, with bodywork by Plaxton or Duple, represented some continuity with what had gone before. However, in terms of appearance it was the coach fleet that was to undergo the most radical change as a result of the imposition of NBC's corporate image.

In 1972 Southdown's coaching operations came under the control of NBC's Central Activities Group, becoming 'National Express' or 'National Holidays' according to the type of service. The livery couldn't have been simpler — all-over white, with no relief. 'NATIONAL' in large alternate red and blue letters together with the double-N symbol were applied towards the rear of the vehicle, and a small red company fleetname above the front wheel arch was the only clue to the operator's identity.

In the early 'Seventies Leyland's inability to meet demand for chassis prompted NBC to order a number of lightweight chassis from Ford and Bedford. Whilst the Bedfords were quite at home in fleets such as Southern Vectis, the 40 Ford R1114s delivered to Southdown in 1974 and 1977 were completely out of place and, like the Commer Avengers of the late 'Fifties, spent much of their lives lurking in the dark corners of depots and yards. Otherwise deliveries in the 'Seventies were of Leyland Leopards with bodywork by either Duple or Plaxton.

Some relief from National white was afforded in 1977 by the delivery, in green and white dual-purpose livery, of the first examples of what Southdown termed 'grant coaches' — effectively full coaches with two-leaf electrically operated doors making them suitable for accruing at least 50% of their annual mileage on stage-carriage services, thereby qualifying for the Government's New Bus Grant. Further variety appeared the same year when six Leopards were outshopped in a striking livery of ultramarine, white and dark orange to the order of ferry operator Townsend Thoresen. One of these would later 'defect' to rival P&O, gaining an attractive pale blue and white. In the meantime three further Leopards wore an even more dramatic livery

of white and various shades of blue, befitting their use as courtesy vehicles connecting with the short-lived Seajet cross-Channel hydrofoil service from Brighton Marina. The coaches in question, delivered in 1978/9, were among Southdown's first to an increased length of 12m, thenceforward adopted as standard for all but 'grant coaches'.

In 1980 Southdown found yet another excuse to resurrect its much-missed traditional coach livery, the first of an eventual seven Plaxton-bodied Leopards appearing in apple green to celebrate the company's 65th anniversary. Appropriately enough the vehicles selected were from the 1971 batch of touring coaches — the last delivered in these colours.

In the early 'Eighties new limited-stop coach services offered yet another opportunity to break away from the NBC livery. Amongst these was the 'Flightline' 777 (Crawley–Gatwick–London), introduced in May 1981 and operated jointly with London Country Bus Services, for which coaches were painted in a green, white and gold livery with dual '**SOUTHDOWN**' and '**GREEN LINE**' fleetnames. Another, also joint with London Country and introduced in May 1982, was the 'Sealine' 773, running between Gatwick, Crawley and Brighton. Southdown's contribution comprised Leopard/Duple 'grant coaches' with 'SEALINE 773' branding added to their existing green/white livery, but in 1983/4 the two regular vehicles gained an attractive livery of two-tone green and white in NBC's so-called 'venetian blind' style, which was by this time appearing in various colour combinations on other Southdown coaches.

Early in 1983, following the withdrawal of a number of National Express services, Southdown took the opportunity to reintroduce its own stopping coach services between the Sussex and Hampshire coastal towns and London. Coaches from the Sussex resorts were branded 'Sussex Link' and given a very attractive livery of white with an apple-green waistband and black and yellow lining. Services from Southsea were similarly branded as 'Solent Link'. The following year Southdown revived the 'South Coast Express' title for a to a limited-stop service (900) from Brighton to Portsmouth, although in truth this was a mere

shadow of the original South Coast Express. Coaches used were painted in another version of NBC's new 'venetian blind' local-coach livery, this time leaf green and white with black and yellow stripes, in a style (known as 'Southdown Universal') that would also be adopted by similar vehicles used on 'Stage Coach' services 727, 737, 770 and 799.

On the vehicle front, the Leyland Leopard formed the basis of new coaches until 1982, the last (car 1367) being delivered in August of that year. Thereafter the standard choice was the Leyland Tiger, Southdown's first (1001) making its debut in April 1983 at the British Coach Rally in a dark-green and gold version of the 'venetian blind' livery that many considered more reminiscent of traditional Maidstone & District colours. Its fellow Southdown entrants in this Brighton-based event were a 1982 Leopard/Plaxton (in a similar livery but with apple green in lieu of the 'M&D' shade) and yet another of the Leopard/Plaxton tourers of 1971, restored to apple green but with the addition of a 'gold' (actually beige) band and named *The Southdown*

The first coaches delivered to Southdown in National white were 15 Duple Dominant-bodied Leyland Leopards that arrived in the spring of 1973. By this time the National Express network was well established, 1258 (CUF 258L) being seen on service 026 at Canterbury when relatively new.
John Bishop / Online Transport Archive

Diplomat. Fitted out as a 15-seater for use as an executive coach, it was joined on such work in 1984 by Southdown's first high-floor coach, a Leyland Tiger/Duple Caribbean 21-seater finished in two-tone brown and white and named *The Statesman*. Four similar vehicles (albeit 50-seaters) arrived the following year to upgrade Southdown's provision on the Flightline 777 service, for which they wore yet another version of the 'venetian blind' livery, this time in apple green with yellow stripes. With the addition of black stripes these colours now spread to a number of touring coaches hitherto in National white. The corporate image was looking vulnerable.

Older coaches looked less comfortable in plain National white. One of a batch of 25 delivered in 1968, Plaxton Panorama-bodied Leopard 1230 (LCD 230F) basks in the sunshine outside Portsmouth's Winston Churchill Avenue depot in April 1978. John Bishop / Online Transport Archive

Among the oldest Southdown coaches to don National white were the Leopard/Panoramas of 1966. Photographed shortly after repainting, 1200 (EUF 200D) emerges from the coach station at Worthing in the early 1970s. Regrettably the building visible on the left has since been demolished, though the depot buildings behind it **survive.** J. Chisholm / Southdown Enthusiasts' Club

The Leyland Leopard/Duple Commander touring coaches of 1967 were not flattered by the application of National white. So treated the previous December, 1788 (HCD 388E) is seen parked in the yard behind Bognor Regis bus station on 16 June 1974. John Bishop / Online Transport Archive

A Leyland Leopard/Duple Commander IV new in 1970, 1810 (RUF 810H) peers through the doors of Hilsea depot in April 1978. Five of this batch had been transferred to fellow NBC subsidiary Alder Valley in 1975, whilst 1810 would be among 12 to pass to Hants & **Dorset in 1981.** John Bishop / Online Transport Archive

In the late 1970s various contract liveries were applied to Southdown coaches. Photographed on Brighton's Madeira Drive in May 1978, Plaxton Supreme-bodied Leopards 1268 and 1269 (LWV 268/9P) were among six such vehicles repainted the previous year for operation on the range of Continental tours run in conjunction with ferry operator **Townsend Thoresen.** John Bishop / Online Transport Archive

The Ford/Duple coaches foisted upon Southdown in the mid-1970s were never popular, and some saw less than five years' service with the company. One of the first batch of 37, delivered in the spring and summer of 1974, 1422 (PUF 262M) is seen outside Chichester garage in April 1978, waiting to depart for Bournemouth on National Express service 026. Lurking inside is Leyland PD2 driver trainer T772 (OCD 772), which has since joined the ranks of preserved Southdown vehicles. John Bishop / Online Transport Archive

During the NBC era the majority of stage-carriage services terminating in Brighton were re-routed away from the town's Pool Valley bus station to serve Churchill Square, while coaches moved in, the coach station in Steine Street closing in the early 1970s. This view, recorded in the late 1970s, features recently delivered Duple-bodied Leyland Leopard 1287 (RYJ 887R) alongside Ford/Duple 1409 (PUF 249M) and East Kent AEC Reliance/Plaxton 8146 (WJG 146J), both on the long National Express route 026. John Bishop / Online Transport Archive

In 1977/8 Southdown took delivery of 17 Leyland Leopards with Duple Dominant I coachwork fitted with power-operated two-leaf doors to facilitate operation on stage-carriage services; as such these vehicles qualified for New Bus Grant (whereby the Government contributed up to 50% of the purchase cost) and came to be known in company circles as 'grant coaches'. One of the first batch of nine, delivered in 'local coach' livery, 1287 (RYJ 887R) brings a touch of luxury to Brighton–East Grinstead route 170 as it waits to depart Pool Valley. John Bishop / Online Transport Archive

Above: **A further 13 'grant coaches', again based on the Leyland Leopard chassis but this time with Plaxton Supreme bodywork, arrived in 1978/9. Looking attractive in leaf green and white as it heads for home on route 180 from Uckfield, Eastbourne's 1306 (ANJ 306T) was photographed in April 1980 in London Road, Hailsham.** John Bishop / Online Transport Archive

Left: **Received in the autumn of 1978, Southdown's first 12m coaches — Leopards with Plaxton Supreme bodywork similar to that on 1306 above — were followed a year later by a quartet bodied by Duple to its handsome Dominant II style. Delivered in National white, they were used primarily on tours and excursion work; so engaged, 1339 (EAP 939V) was photographed in September 1980 negotiating the narrow bridge at Cuckmere Haven on the main A259 Eastbourne–Brighton road. In the background can just be discerned a Bristol VR toiling up Exceat Hill on its way to Eastbourne on route 112.** John Bishop / Online Transport Archive

Left: **Discounting vehicles painted for specific tours contracts, one of the first coach liveries to break away from National white was that applied in April 1981 to two newly delivered Plaxton Supreme IV-bodied Leopards used on the 'Flightline' 777 service between London and Gatwick Airport. The livery of white, leaf green and gold was in fact an adaptation of that devised by fellow NBC subsidiary London Country for the 50th anniversary of Green Line, with which the route was shared. With dual 'GREEN LINE' and 'SOUTHDOWN' fleetnames (the former writ larger than the latter!), an immaculate 1341 (MAP 341W) is seen inside Brighton's Freshfield Road coach depot in May 1981. Southdown's contribution would be doubled early the following year, at which point the disparity in fleetnames was corrected.** John Bishop / Online Transport Archive

Above: **The withdrawal of certain National Express workings prompted the introduction early in 1983 of 'Sussexlink' and 'Solentlink' express services between London and the South Coast. The vehicles used, Plaxton Supreme IV-bodied Leopards new in 1980, were painted in an attractive livery of white with a broad waistband in Southdown green, surmounted by a black/yellow stripe; the skirt was dark green. Seen at Kingston-on-Thames on 10 June 1984 is 'Sussexlink' 1325 (GWV 925V) on route S67 from Chichester.** Gerald Mead

Below left: **In the spring of 1980 Southdown used its 65th anniversary as an excuse to repaint two coaches in traditional livery. Appropriately the vehicles in question were chosen from the 1971 batch of Plaxton Panorama Elite-bodied Leopards, the last coaches delivered before the introduction of National white. As the decade progressed, further examples appeared in green, such that by 1982 no fewer than eight were so adorned. This photograph shows 1835 (UUF 335J) resplendent at Eastbourne's Cavendish Place coach station, the overall effect marred only by the red and blue seating from a later vehicle. Providing a stark contrast is a sorry-looking 3113 (NUF 452G), formerly 452, one of the dual-purpose Northern Counties-bodied Leopards of 1969, by now seeing out its days as a left-luggage office.** John Bishop / Online Transport Archive

Right: From the early 1980s coaches were allocated more specifically to particular types of work, and to reflect this the National white livery evolved in two directions. From 1982 coaches used on National Holidays work, identified latterly by appropriate fleetnames in NBC's standard typeface, adopted this less restrained style, seen on a Southdown Leopard/ Plaxton Supreme of 1976. One of three such vehicles extensively refurbished over the winter of 1984/5, 1276 (OWV 276R) gained a Supreme V-style lower front and a 'dateless' registration that was rightfully the property of a 1964 Leyland PD3, both alterations being intended to conceal its nine years. Photographed taking part in the 1985 British Coach Rally on 20 April, it was about to leave Crawley on the road run to Brighton. Note the small 'SOUTHDOWN' fleetname in grey beneath the driver's side window. Brian Jackson / Southdown Enthusiasts' Club

Right: From 1983 coaches used on National Express work began to appear in a more dramatic livery of white with matt-black window-surrounds and red and blue stripes applied in a style that was soon likened to a venetian blind. Among the Southdown vehicles so treated were a number of the 'grant coaches' that had been new in green and white. Leopard/Duple 1286 (RYJ 886R) was nevertheless back on stage-carriage duties on 7 September 1985, being pictured at Etchingham (near the Kent/Sussex border) on 'day out' service 718 from Brighton to Canterbury. Paul Gainsbury / Southdown Enthusiasts' Club

Right: In 1985 touring coaches not dedicated to specific duties began to forsake National white in favour of an attractive scheme featuring Southdown green with yellow and black stripes and 'SOUTHDOWN' fleetnames. Of the quartet of Duple-bodied 12m Leopards delivered in 1979 the only one to receive these colours was Chichester's 1338 (EAP 938V), seen outside its home garage in the spring of 1986. Eagle-eyed readers will have noticed that on both this coach and 1286 above the grille/headlight assembly has been re-fitted upside-down, with the result that the NBC logo now points the wrong way. Calvin Churchill / Southdown Enthusiasts' Club

Left: **In April 1983 Southdown took delivery of its first new Leyland Tiger since 1949, the name having been revived for a chassis that was ultimately to replace the Leopard in the manufacturer's model range. Appropriately starting a new number series, 1001 (XUF 531Y) was the first of five fitted with Plaxton's new Paramount body and delivered in a handsome livery of white, dark green and gold applied in 'venetian blind' style.** Southdown Enthusiasts' Club

Below left: **Likely to confuse the unwary was Southdown 1358 (LPN 358W), a 12m Leyland Leopard delivered in April 1981. In 1983 its original Plaxton Supreme IV body was destroyed in an arson attack, and it reappeared the following year with a new Plaxton Paramount body of the style by then being fitted to new Leyland Tigers such as 1001 above. Painted in Southdown's attractive green, yellow and black version of NBC's 'venetian blind' livery, it is seen on Brighton's Madeira Drive at the rally held in June 1985 to celebrate the company's 70th anniversary. In 1987 it would be fitted with a Leyland TL11 engine, such that it not only looked but sounded like a Tiger, the deception being completed when its W-suffix registration (too early for a Paramount) was replaced by a 'dateless' mark (408 DCD) that once graced a Leyland PD3.** Southdown Enthusiasts' Club

Left: **The 1984 delivery of Leyland Tigers included six with Duple's curvaceous Laser bodywork, all of which were used initially on National Holidays work. Still on trade plates, a newly delivered 1011 (A811 CCD) is seen in Eastbourne's Cavendish Place coach station. Sadly the coach station and depot are no more, but 1011 has been saved for preservation.** Paul Gainsbury / Southdown Enthusiasts' Club

The seventh Tiger delivered in 1984 was fitted with high-floor Duple Caribbean bodywork and had just 21 seats, being fitted out as an executive coach with tables, servery and a toilet. Received in January, 1184 (A184 EWV) made its debut as *The Statesman* at the 30th British Coach Rally in April, being seen on Brighton's Madeira Drive in an unusual version of 'venetian blind' livery with stripes in two shades of brown. Its out-of-sequence fleet number was allocated to match its registration, which was expected to be replaced by a 'dateless' mark, although by the time this happened (in 1988) the coach had long since been upseated and reliveried for more general work. Calvin Churchill / Southdown Enthusiasts' Club

In 1985 four similar vehicles with Duple's facelifted Caribbean II coachwork (and fitted with 50 seats) were delivered to update Southdown's contribution to the 'Flightline' 777 service between Gatwick Airport and London. Seen approaching Victoria Coach Station on 29 June is 1012 (B812 JPN). The livery was yet another version of the 'venetian blind' style, the stripes this time being in Southdown green and yellow. Calvin Churchill / Southdown Enthusiasts' Club

6

THE BEGINNING OF THE END

A S SOUTHDOWN prepared to celebrate its 70th anniversary in 1985 major changes were on the cards with the impending deregulation of the bus-operating industry and privatisation of the National Bus Company. A Government White Paper to this effect had been published the previous year, and in a bid to stave off its demise NBC was now encouraging its subsidiaries to become more locally accountable. Thus, with effect from 1 March 1985, Southdown established four operating divisions — Hampshire, West Sussex, East & Mid Sussex and Brighton & Hove — plus an engineering division based at Portslade Works.

In May 1985 NBC proposed that the newly created divisions be segregated as self-contained operating companies. This was resisted by Southdown's management, but in August of that year it was decided that the Brighton & Hove division should become a separate company, to be formed by reactivating the dormant Brighton, Hove & District Omnibus Co Ltd. The engineering division also would be set up as a company in its own right — Southdown Engineering Services Ltd — but the remainder of the operation was to continue as Southdown Motor Services Ltd.

By now Southdown's operating divisions were experimenting with their own identities — Hampshire with more white on its double-deckers, West Sussex with unrelieved leaf green on its single-deckers and, most visibly, East & Mid Sussex with a near-traditional application of apple green and cream; the last two also introduced subsidiary divisional fleetnames.

At Brighton & Hove a handful of buses emerged from repaint still in leaf green and white but with dual '**SOUTHDOWN**' and '**BRIGHTON & HOVE**' fleetnames, the latter noticeably larger than the former. However, the impending 50th anniversary of BH&D served as a catalyst for a resurgence of red and cream, which was applied in traditional style to three Leyland Nationals. Thus began a series of experiments to decide upon a livery for the 'new' Brighton & Hove company. Two VRs — one a convertible open-topper, the other an older bus used largely on contract work — appeared in cream with an apple-green waistband, another convertible in cream with a red band, and — best of all — a dual-door example in traditional BH&D red and cream. All had NBC-style fleetnames but in colours appropriate to the livery — green, red or gold. In the event none of these was chosen, the new company opting for a more contemporary application of its traditional colours, with a 'Brighton & Hove' fleetname in black upper- and lower-case lettering.

In May 1985 the newly created East & Mid Sussex division had convertible-open-top Bristol VR 620 (UWV 620S) repainted in this attractive livery of Southdown green and white, with appropriate fleetnames; note also the 'Southdown 70' logo, although the NBC double N still appears on the front. Freshly outshopped, the bus is seen waiting to depart Princes Road, Eastbourne, for Beachy Head. John Bishop / Online Transport Archive

The forthcoming changes would affect not only the vehicles and services but also the buildings. The ex-BH&D garages at Conway Street and Whitehawk would pass, naturally, to Brighton & Hove, but as the new company would have a larger sphere of operations than had the original BH&D and would also encompass coaching activities it also took over the truly 'Southdown' garages at Moulsecoomb and Freshfield Road. Adjoining the latter was Southdown House, the company's head office since 1964, but with Brighton & Hove reverting to BH&D's traditional HQ at Conway Street and Southdown vacating Brighton altogether this found itself surplus to requirements, and in 1986 a much smaller Southdown would move into more modest premises in Lewes.

New vehicles delivered prior to the partition of the company included eight late-model Leyland National 2s (the first since 1981, and this time with Gardner engines), all of which were allocated to the Brighton & Hove division. Six, diverted from Blackpool Transport, arrived in plain white, and four of these entered service thus in September 1985 on the Mile Oak Shuttle, displacing some of the Bristol VRs used thereon; the other four were among the first vehicles treated to the new Brighton & Hove livery and entered service in November, initially on longer-distance services.

Meanwhile the Hampshire division received a striking new coach that broke Southdown's allegiance to Leyland, being a Hestair-Duple 425 integral. This wore yet another new livery, of silver with diagonal apple-green stripes and '**SOUTHDOWN COACHES**' fleetnames. The vehicle was to remain unique within the fleet, although the livery — in modified form with white as the base colour — quickly spread to other Portsmouth-based coaches.

The only other vehicles delivered before the end of 1985 were 13 Mercedes-Benz minibuses, which arrived in base coat of pale cream and passed unused to the Brighton & Hove company. Early in 1986, however, Southdown itself received the first of 16 similar vehicles in a livery of green and yellow. Embellished with the addition of 'Southdown MiniBus' fleetnames (the company name being in Mackenzie script!), these were allocated to the East & Mid Sussex division, entering service at Eastbourne and Haywards Heath. The last new full-size vehicles to be delivered to Southdown in the NBC era were a trio of Plaxton-bodied Leyland Tiger coaches that entered service from Portsmouth, initially on National Express work, in the spring of 1986. Thereafter the only acquisitions arrived second-hand from other NBC subsidiaries. In the main comprising Leyland Nationals and Bristol VRs, these generally entered service in the liveries of their previous operators — unthinkable in even the recent past. Gradually, however, most gained a coat of green and cream, which by the end of 1986 had been adopted by all three divisions, West Sussex buses additionally gaining a dark-green skirt. Early in 1987 the divisional structure was abandoned, and the fleet once again began to take on a unified appearance. The stage was set for privatisation.

Southdown Engineering Services became the first of the Southdown 'subsidiaries' to be sold, passing on 5 March 1987 to Frontsource, part of the Robert Beattie group. Brighton & Hove was sold to its management on 8 May, Southdown similarly on 2 October. The NBC days were over.

Left: **In the spring of 1985 the Brighton & Hove division experimented with various combinations of red and cream and green and cream. In May Bristol VR 523 (WCD 523K), largely relegated to contract work, appeared in this attractive version of cream with waistband and skirt in Southdown green. It was followed by a pair of convertible open-toppers, one of which featured red in lieu of green. However, such experiments were overtaken by events, and with the news that the dormant BH&D company was to be reactivated as a separate subsidiary within NBC (itself now doomed) the Brighton & Hove division would settle on a more contemporary application of red and cream with a style of fleetname that bore no relation to NBC's corporate image.** Calvin Churchill / Southdown Enthusiasts' Club

Left: **Southdown's last new Leyland Nationals were eight late-model National 2s that arrived for the Brighton & Hove division in the summer and autumn of 1985. One of four placed in service in overall white on the Mile Oak 'Shuttle' (releasing four of that route's orange Bristol VRs for repaint in the new Brighton & Hove livery), 152 (C452 OAP) was photographed in the Old Steine on 17 October.** Paul Gainsbury / Southdown Enthusiasts' Club

Left: **Following a period of repainting its single-deckers in unrelieved leaf green, the West Sussex division in 1986 adopted an attractive version of traditional Southdown colours, including a dark-green skirt, as well as Southdown's new 'S' logo. Seen the following year departing Worthing depot is 91 (AYJ 91T), a Leyland National new in 1979.** John Bishop / Online Transport Archive

Southdown's Hampshire division initially retained leaf green, although its double-deckers began to appear with a greater area of white between the decks. Leyland Atlantean 708 (PUF 138M) is seen at Cosham on 11 March 1986. *Calvin Churchill / Southdown Enthusiasts' Club*

Possibly the most distinctive coach ever operated by Southdown was a Hestair-Duple 425 integral, 1016 (C716 NYJ), delivered to the Hampshire division in November 1985. It is seen arriving at Epsom Downs on an outing to The Derby on 4 June 1986, still in its striking livery of silver and green, although by now it had been renumbered 1185 to make way for a final trio of Leyland Tigers (also for Portsmouth), delivered that spring. Destined to remain unique in the fleet, it would soon be repainted in National Express livery, but the Southdown Coaches scheme, in a more insipid form with white in lieu of silver, was applied meanwhile to the majority of the Hampshire coach fleet. *Paul Gainsbury / Southdown Enthusiasts' Club*

Right: **In 1985 the 'Solentlink' and most of the 'Sussexlink' routes were discontinued, the coaches used thereon being repainted in the latest National Express livery. By January 1987 Leyland Leopard/ Plaxton 1328 (GWV 928V) was allocated to the East & Mid Sussex division and when photographed in Hailsham High Street had been pressed into stage-carriage service. The year was to see the abandonment of the company's divisional structure and the decimation of the coach fleet, this vehicle, transferred to Portsmouth, being among the survivors.** John Bishop / Online Transport Archive

Right: **One of the last acts of the National Bus Company was to purchase a large number of 'end of line' Ford Transit and Mercedes-Benz parcel vans, which were converted to minibuses and distributed amongst its subsidiaries. Sixteen of the latter type were allocated to Southdown for use at Eastbourne and Haywards Heath. No 904 (C584 SHC), converted by Reeve-Burgess, is seen in Terminus Road, Eastbourne in August 1986. These 'bread vans', as they soon became known, were almost as unpopular amongst enthusiasts as had been the introduction of the corporate livery, so maybe NBC had the last laugh after all!** John Bishop / Online Transport Archive

Right: **One of a diminishing number of vehicles still in NBC leaf green, 136 (RUF 436X), a Leyland National 2 dating from 1981 and recently transferred from Chichester, pauses on Worthing seafront in June 1987. At this time Southdown was still part of NBC, but Brighton & Hove (as the reactivated BH&D now styled itself), represented here by newer National 2 154 (C454 OAP) in that company's new livery, was not, having been sold to its management in May. Southdown would be similarly privatised in October, bringing to a close the company's NBC days.** John Bishop / Online Transport Archive

80

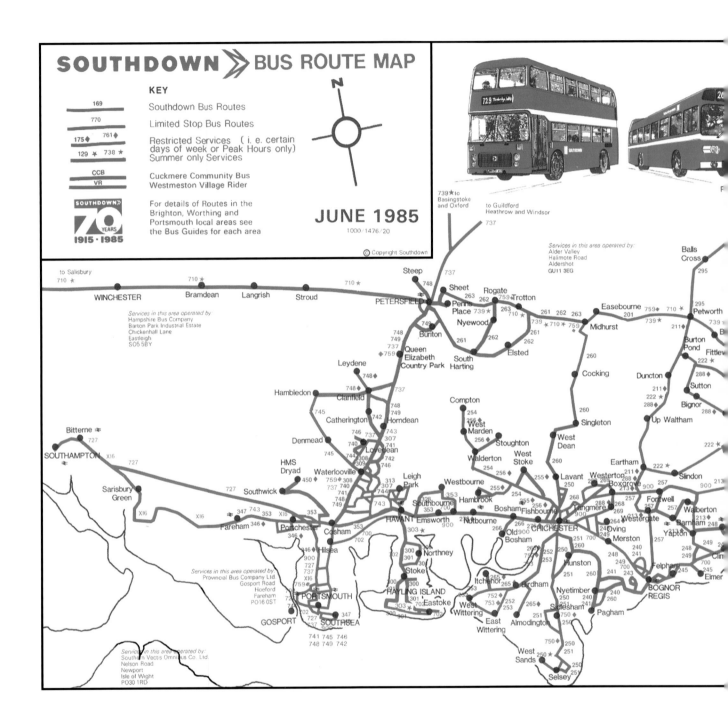

SOUTHDOWN ≫ BUS ROUTE MAP

KEY

169 — Southdown Bus Routes

770 — Limited Stop Bus Routes

175◆ 761◆
129 ✱ 738 ✱ — Restricted Services (i. e. certain days of week or Peak Hours only) Summer only Services

CCB
VR — Cuckmere Community Bus
Westmeston Village Rider

SOUTHDOWN 70 YEARS 1915·1985

For details of Routes in the Brighton, Worthing and Portsmouth local areas see the Bus Guides for each area

JUNE 1985

1000/1476/20

© Copyright Southdown

739✱to Basingstoke and Oxford
to Guildford Heathrow and Windsor
737

Services in this area operated by:
Alder Valley
Halimote Road
Aldershot
GU11 3EG

to Salisbury
710 ✱
WINCHESTER   710 ✱ Bramdean   Langrish   Stroud   710 ✱

Services in this area operated by:
Hampshire Bus Company
Barton Park Industrial Estate
Chickenhall Lane
Eastleigh
SO5 5BY

Steep
737
748
PETERSFIELD   Sheet   Rogate
Penns Place 739✱   263   262 759 Trotton
Nyewood   739   261 262 263   Easebourne 759 710 ✱   Balls Cross
710 ★   263   295
Buriton   749   261   262   261   Midhurst   201   739✱   295 Petworth
737   262   Elsted   260   739✱
759   Queen Elizabeth Country Park   South Harting   211◆   Burton Pond   Fittlew
Leydene   748◆   Cocking   Duncton   222 ✱
748   Hambledon   737   Compton   254   256   260   Singleton   288◆   Sutton
Clanfield   748   West Marden   256 ◆ Stoughton   West Dean   211◆ 222✱ 288◆   Bignor   288◆
Catherington 742 Horndean   749   256   West   Up Waltham
745   743   Walderton   Stoke   West   Eartham   222 ✱
Denmead   746 737 307   741   254   256 ◆   260   Lavant   Westerton   Slindon
Bitterne ≠   740   308 742   Westbourne   255◆   255◆   250   288◆ Boxgrove   900   222 ✱
727   744 746   Leigh   353   254   Fontwell   257   900
SOUTHAMPTON   HMS Dryad   Lovedean   Park   313   Hambrook   255   256   268 257   Walberton   213✱
X16   450◆ 759 308   307   Southbourne   Bosham   255   288◆ 268   Westergate   213◆ 248
Sarisbury Green   727   737 740   744   353   255   Tangmere   264 257   Barnham 248
X16   Southwick   748   743   Emsworth   900   Old 900   249 Oving   257   Yapton   700
347 743 353   749   Havant   303 ★   266   266   CHICHESTER   240   248
Fareham 346◆   Portchester   Cosham   700   Nutbourne   266   Bosham   252   260   Merston   241   249
346◆   346   702   Northney   300   305   900   Old 900   249   Felph   245
727   Hilsea   301   Stoke   Hunston   251   260   241 243   700
900   737   300   Itchenor   265   Birdham   Nyetimer   240   Elmer
759   PORTSMOUTH   301   HAYLING ISLAND   753◆   252   265◆   250   241   BOGNOR REGIS
GOSPORT   727 347   303 ★ 702 Eastoke   West Wittering   753◆ 252   Sidlesham   750◆   Pagham
702   SOUTHSEA   300 301   East Wittering   251   Almodington   250
741 745 746   748 749 742   750◆   250 251
West Sands   250 ★   250   251
Selsey

Services in this area operated by:
Provincial Bus Company Ltd.
Gosport Road
Hoeford
Fareham
PO16 0ST

Services in this area operated by:
Southern Vectis Omnibus Co. Ltd.
Nelson Road
Newport
Isle of Wight
PO30 1RD